STUDYING VIDEOGAMES
BY
JULIAN M^cDOUGALL
& WAYNE O'BRIEN

auteur

First published in 2008 by
Auteur
The Old Surgery, 9 Pulford Road, Leighton Buzzard LU7 1AB
www.auteur.co.uk

Designed and set by Nikki Hamlett at AMP Ltd, Dunstable, Bedfordshire
Cover image *Grand Theft Auto 3* © Rockstar Games
Printed and bound in Poland
www.polskabook.co.uk

British Library Cataloguing-in-Publication Data
A catalogue record for this book is available from the British Library

ISBN 978-1-903663-84-4 (paperback)
ISBN 978-1-903663-85-1 (hardback)

CONTENTS

ACKNOWLEDGEMENTS & DEDICATIONS

Julian would like to pay tribute to the late Jacquie Bennett, a great loss to games education, who provided invaluable guidance on *Second Life* for this book. And to thank Lydia for DS expertise; Alex for literacy expertise; Ned for indiscriminately shouting 'digger'; Pete Fraser, Barney Oram, David Buckingham, David Gauntlett, Steve Dixon, Dave Trotman and Yahya Nakeeb for support; John Atkinson for patience and enthusiasm; and Leverton and Hall's Cafe, Bournville for breakfasts.

Dedicated to Mike McDougall.

Wayne would like to thank Richard Carter and John Foster from Sony Computer Entertainment Europe and to Ian Dean, editor of *PSW magazine* for taking the time to contribute.

For Maxine and the re-introduction to videogames and for Caitlin, one of the next generation of gamers.

The publisher thanks Tom Cabot (www.ketchup-productions.co.uk) for his assistance in the completion of this project.

INTRODUCTION

WHAT ARE VIDEOGAMES?

Just before the publication of this book, the release of *Grand Theft Auto IV* looked set to out-hype even the most heavily promoted Hollywood blockbuster. This confirms three things: Firstly, the videogame industry is set to get even bigger and the broader entertainment business is going to be looking for ever-more opportunities to develop and target this market. Secondly, the controversy over videogames is not going away. The *Grand Theft Auto* series is the most 'worried about' videogame franchise we have seen, but interest in the product continues to grow with each release despite (or maybe because of) supposed public anxiety over its content. And, thirdly, this launch also serves to confirm why it is that such academic courses as Media Studies, English, Communications, IT, Art and Sociology have decided to incorporate videogames into the curriculum - because a game like *GTA IV* needs analysis, explanation and research, so we can understand why it is so popular and what difference it makes to our society. Which is why you are reading this book.

In this book we use the term videogames to describe games played through computers or consoles that feature a screen. But beyond that it gets tricky. Here are two extracts from player reviews of games both released at the time of writing this introduction (posted on www.gamespot.com and accessed on 5.3.7). The first one is for *Zoo Tycoon 2* (Microsoft, 2007):

> One of the first features that I appreciated was the fact that my kids (age 11 & 8) were able to play the game and create a zoo. The construction of a zoo in the free play section of the game is pretty straight forward and not complicated. My kids were able to start creating zoos with very little help from me after the initial tutorial and explanation. It also contains very good graphics, and we enjoyed seeing it as it took shape. There is enough management that can occur behind the scenes to keep me

interested as well. Starting the career path was enjoyable for me. It gave me the chance to create zoos from scratch given a limited budget and criteria that needed to be accomplished. I found it challenging yet enjoyable to play the game.

And the second is for *The Grim Adventures of Billy and Mandy* (Midway, 2007):

The gameplay in *Billy and Mandy* is simple. You choose one of the 15 playable characters and beat the living crap out of up to three other characters at a time. You have anywhere from one to four lives going into battle, and when you lose all of your lives you're out of the match. Each character has a weak attack and a slower, harder-to-pull-off strong attack. In addition, each character has a couple of special 'mojo' attacks. As you fight you'll find and collect mojo balls, which fill up your mojo meter. Once it's full, you can perform a mojo smackdown, which is a series of attacks that automatically hit for heavy damage. If you fill up your mojo meter two times over, you can do a mojo meltdown attack. When you pull off a mojo meltdown the camera will zoom in on the action and a series of button icons will appear on the screen. If you press the corresponding buttons in time, you'll instantly kill your opponent. If you're playing the Wii version of the game, instead of pressing buttons you have to aim the Wii Remote at targets that randomly appear onscreen. Aside from that the only difference in the Wii version of the game is that to perform a strong attack you have to shake the Wii Remote instead of pressing a button.

Although these two games were randomly chosen from the thousands on new release, they help us to establish some context for this book. One game is being discussed by a parent who has a clear sense of the educational potential of games. The game in question is a simulation, and teachers and parents are increasingly aware of the possibilities this genre of game offers for learning. The second is a 'kill or be killed' game, the likes of which are often blamed for an alleged decline in the moral values, social skills and even health of young people. The reviewer is critical of the fact that the Wii version of the game is not very different and thus the kinaesthetic pleasures that this new console offers are not being fully utilised.

Two very different games and two very different critical perspectives. If you put into the equation a range of other very different types of games – from *Championship Manager* to *Wipeout* to *Sing Star* you can start to see where this is going – it's hard to pin down what we mean by a videogame and how we analyse it will depend on what we are looking at. An 'academic' response to a game will be different to a player review. But even the two player reviews above come from contrasting points of view. That's the problem with studying videogames – it all depends on how you want to judge them:

Games are good at novelistic storytelling the way Michael Jordan was good at playing baseball. Both could probably make a living out of it, but their world-class talents lie elsewhere. (Johnson, 2005: 21)

PLAYING / READING

One thing is clear – the way that we consume games is profoundly different to how we consume other media. Understanding a media text, whether it's a film, TV show, piece of music, magazine or website is never passive. We always make the meaning ourselves according to our own cultural experiences and ways of understanding 'reality' (whatever that might be). But with a videogame it is more complex because we play the game in order to read it. We are in the story ourselves either through an avatar (the on-screen representation of the player) which we have been given, one we have designed or we might appear ourselves on the screen. If you consider the huge range of games available, then to say you are 'in the story' could mean that you are being C.J. (Carl Johnson) in *Grand Theft Auto: San Andreas*; or that you are being the owner of a Labrador you have customised in *Nintendogs*; or that you are playing tennis against your friend with Nintendo Wii, in which case it really will be you on the screen. Then again, C.J. is really you in so much as you are controlling him and seeing the (virtual) world through his eyes. So it is all mixed up, and this book will help you analyse this complexity using some of the Media Studies concepts you can use for other media (such as genre, narrative and representation) and some new concepts that we need for videogames specifically (like ludology – a theory which helps us look at the dynamics of play in games).

WHO IS THIS BOOK FOR?

Just as we have established the variety of games out there, so there are a range of ways you can study them. For Media Studies, the onus is on analysis - of individual games, the games industry or a range of games within a theoretical debate such as postmodern media. There are also options to design games for coursework. Vocational diplomas include units on games design which are more practical. And other academic subjects are dealing with games as texts or as programmes, models and environments. This book will be of use to any student who needs to develop an informed theoretical approach to deconstructing games (pulling them apart to see how they work) alongside a factual knowledge of how designers and corporations produce them and how the games work in technological terms. This will be equally important to a games design student – after all, creativity is sparked when theory and practice meet.

> A videogame must provide novel or exciting situations to experience, stimulating puzzles to engage with, and interesting environments to explore. Moreover, it must offer the player not merely suitable or appropriate capabilities, but capabilities that can be earned, honed and perfected. (Newman, 2004:16)

This book has virtually (pardon the pun) no chance of competing with a game for this kind of engagement, but we will do our best to provide some interesting new terrain for you to navigate.

GAMES STUDIES

In this book, we begin by analysing a range of games using media concepts and looking at the language of games. We test out tools like genre, narrative, representation, ideology and audience, alongside ludology, interactivity, structure, rule systems, game design principles, identity, engagement and agency. This also includes some questions about online community 'worlds' such as *Second Life*. Are these games or 'experiences', or both? We are constrained, of course, by the pace of change. By the time you read this many new games and new platforms will have moved these debates forward, so the approaches offered are flexible enough for you to apply them to new examples of your own. Along the way, you will consider games as texts that might challenge us to rethink what we mean by literacy, by reading. Look at this statement made in an interview by the American media educator Steve Goodman:

> So much information in our society now originates outside of the classroom, through mass media. That includes films, TV, billboards, magazines, as well as the more interactive variety – the internet, and websites and computer games. I think that kids have to learn to critically read those media that are visual, aural, as well as print. I'd like to see them able to be fluent in writing and creating and authoring those media and to be full participants in the culture. (in Tyner, 1998: 244)

So studying games is about more than just comparing them to other kinds of narrative or being able to understand how they work in design terms. It's also about contributing to a debate about what it means to be literate in the twenty-first century. Whilst some are derisory about text language, blogging and gaming – thinking of these as deficient forms of communication when compared to more traditional ways of reading and writing – others see an increase in 'multimodal' literacy brought about by new technologies, social networking and games that require the player to take on a new identity. It's all up for discussion.

Next we explore the history of games development and the various audience groups for games. We find that the stereotype of the lone male, teenage gamer locked in a bedroom is a myth and that much gaming is social (and that the average gamer is older than many people think). Here we delve into the workings of the games industry and how multinational corporations compete for this immense market. We also look to the future and offer some designer perspectives on the next generation of games.

> New research, carried out by scientists at the University of Missouri-Columbia, goes some way towards demonstrating a causal link between computer games and violence, rather than a simple association. When shown images of real-life violence, people who played violent video games were found to have a diminished brain response. However, the same group had more natural reactions to other emotionally disturbing images, such as those of dead animals or ill children. (Lister, 2006; *Chicago Times*)

As this example illustrates, games are rarely discussed in neutral terms. This is an emotive subject. In the following chapter, then, the huge debate about the 'effects' of games is weighed up. We look at the range of 'moral panics' set in motion by allegations of negative influence (some more plausible than others). These debates are put in dialogue with the 'educational agenda' for games and cognitive development, and we consider a range of research which has led to bold claims for the potential of videogames to revolutionise education in the future. On the other hand, games and other electronic media are increasingly blamed for a 'childhood obesity epidemic' and we analyse these claims too. At the end of this section of the book, you will need to form your own opinion, but whatever view you take, you will be entering the debate from a well-informed vantage point.

Having established a range of ways of looking at games that we might call a general 'games studies' approach, the final chapter applies all of these perspectives to a specific games series – *Grand Theft Auto*. Here we offer an extended case study, deconstructing the series in terms of design, commercial product, text and 'effects'.

Finally, we offer a 'toolkit' for applying your new understanding in the form of a glossary of technical / academic terms and a comprehensive list of web resources and further reading.

How you apply the framework we offer here will depend on the context in which you are studying games. And it goes without saying that in years to come people will write books (or whatever replaces them) about particular types of games or aspects of them. This is an early contribution to a rapidly developing academic field, but as Media, English, Communications, Art, IT, Psychology and Sociology courses start to include videogames within the curriculum, we hope this book can act as a useful starting point and help you to take games seriously.

Julian McDougall and Wayne O'Brien

1. GAMES AND MEDIA CONCEPTS

When we study individual media texts, the approach we take is normally textual analysis. This is borrowed, in part, from the study of literature and other cultural forms, which is one reason why so many Media teachers have an English degree. But whether or not this will work for videogames is up for grabs. Burn, Carr and Schott explain why:

'Some theorists argue that an account of a digital game that focuses solely on the game as a "text" will be incomplete. Because digital games employ the power of computers, they are able to generate multiple responses to input from their users. The way that Lara Croft acts when one person plays her might vary a great deal from the ways that she moves or acts when another person is at the controls. This is why theories drawn from older media (film or literature for example) can't fully describe digital games. Games also complicate old notions about the relationship between authors and readers, because players determine how the "hero" behaves. By compiling and distributing software modifications and cheats, gamers also disrupt the distinctions between the games producers and its consumers.' (Burn, Carr and Schott, 2003: 10)

If Lara Croft is before your time, substitute her name for a main character / avatar in a game you are playing at the moment. The point is that along the way here we might need to create our own theories, if, like Burn, Carr and Schott, we don't feel entirely comfortable with the ability of the 'classic concepts' to adapt to these interactive products.

So in this chapter we will do two things. The one is easier than the other. Firstly, we will take the conceptual framework we use for Media Studies generally and apply it to this relatively new media form. This will involve deconstructing a range of games to see how they use **media language** to make meaning for players, how they work in terms of their **genre** conventions, their **narrative** structures and themes, the ways in which they **represent** people and ideas (and reality itself), and the ways in which **audiences** respond to them and are constructed by them. This will also take us to an analysis of how these elements combine to produce a range of **ideological** meanings. Straightforward enough – at this level we are dismantling videogames with a tried and tested analytical toolkit, just as we might do with other media forms like films, television programmes, magazines and newspapers.

But it isn't that simple. A range of writers, games designers and researchers have suggested that these concepts don't really work for games; or, if they do, then only up to a point. So secondly, we will consider this debate and look at the limitations of each concept for games analysis, as well as thinking about some alternative concepts such as immersion, ludology and flow.

First it is essential that we state something pretty obvious. There are so many types of game that it actually makes little sense to try to formulate theoretical approaches to all of them. We think this is more the case for games than it is for other media forms. *The Sun* newspaper looks and reads a lot different to *The New York Times*, but you can use analytical ideas like news agenda, layout, ideology, representation and narrative to compare them. The same is true for highly contrasting television programmes like *Newsnight* and *Wife Swap* – both have a narrative, both have *mise-en-scène*, both are clearly representational texts. And we can also do this with two very different films, like *Kill Bill Vol. 2* (2004) and *Vera Drake* (2004) – genre, narrative, represention, *mise-en-scène*, audience – they all work for both, and for comparing them. But when it comes to videogames, can we find concepts that will help us compare *SingStar*, tennis on the Wii and *Grand Theft Auto*? *Championship Manager*, *Brain Trainer* and *Masterclass Chess* alongside *Silent Hill*, *Mortal Kombat* and *Resident Evil*? *Second Life* and *Space Invaders*? We are pretty sure that in the near future there will be a range of study guides to different types of game, which won't have this problem. But for now, we are stuck with the mind boggling variety of game types that Newman and Oram describe:

> 'It is not surprising that there is no easy or agreed answer to the question – what is a videogame? Even attempting to define videogames in terms of their differences from other media, entertainments or forms is a complex task. In a sense "videogames" are the things that videogame players play. Indeed it is possible to play with things that are not labelled as games per se. It is common to be extremely and self-consciously non-productive and playful with productivity software such as Microsoft Word or Excel – playing with formatting, exploring the capabilities and varies of the application, perhaps even trying to make it crash – so is Microsoft Office a videogame? Surely, we would baulk at any definition that allowed these titles to be included but we play them on the same device and with the same interface of mouse, keyboard and display, as *Half Life 2*. It is useful to consider our presuppositions about what videogames are and are not by questioning why the DVD version of *Who Wants to be a Millionaire?* or a Tamagotchi virtual pet should or should not be included in our definition of "videogames".' (Newman and Oram: 2006: 9)

Readers of this book will probably choose to look at the kinds of game that work most easily for their course. Students on courses with a production emphasis will be making games, and so they will be 'theorising' their own game designs as well as, or instead of, the existing commercial ones. So what follows is a set of analytical 'ways in' to studying any type of game. But we urge you to embrace the '*jouissance*' that comes with difficult study like this – you may find you are asking more questions than finding answers.

Bruce (2002) offers an acronym – 'MIGRAIN' – for studying any media text, which looks like this:

MEDIA LANGUAGE

INSTITUTION

GENRE

REPRESENTATION

AUDIENCE

IDEOLOGY

NARRATIVE

If we apply this acronym straightforwardly to a game, in this case *Medal of Honor,* we can come up with this kind of analysis:

MEDIA LANGUAGE: Looking at the construction of verisimilitude through *mise-en-scène*, the *Medal of Honor* series offers intertextual references to *Saving Private Ryan* (1998) and seeks to establish a recognition by the gamer of a learned sense of the 'look' of World War II from the Allies' perspective.

INSTITUTION: Video games are part of a hugely competitive and lucrative market, and the companies that distribute them are convergent entities. Microsoft, Nintendo and Sony are fighting a battle for control of this market, and games designers operate in the midst of these turf-wars. Designers have their own styles, and most games have a great deal of intertextual franchise elements for us to analyse.

GENRE: This is a refreshing area when compared to traditional Media learning, since there are no 'tried and tested' resources packs on this genre or that. As a result, discussions are more organic and negotiation of genre labelling can happen 'live'. The relationship between genre as subject matter (e.g. football games) and format for the player (e.g. single player) is an interesting, transformative area for study. Whether online gaming is a genre or a technological development might also be considered.

REPRESENTATION: All media learning is really about representation and the other concepts are merely roads to this destination. Key questions are to do with the viewer / reader / player identities – who is good and bad; how are nations, genders, occupations, societies, species, real personalities represented; which dominant discourses are circulated; and crucially, if I am in the game, am I represented, or do I take on another represented identity? What power do I have to negotiate this role? Am I inside or outside of the text and its representational devices?

AUDIENCE: We cannot get into this kind of work without researching our peers as audience members. Who is playing what games, and in what context (online, solitary, with friends)? What pleasures are obtained? What connections with other media pleasures are evident? Is the audience really a kind of 'learning community' (see Gee, 2003)? What does student research offer in response to the popular assumptions about gaming and the attendant moral panics?

IDEOLOGY: This is the area that demands the most caution. If we just state that *Medal of Honor* represents a horribly crude, simplified, American mis-remembering of World War II and as such is firmly entrenched in a Bush era dominant ideology of cultural imperialism masquerading as the 'spreading' of democracy, we might be pretty justified; but this is a particular view informed by an English historical perspective. As such it is not ideologically neutral. The more interesting work is to do with game players' perceptions of their identity within the game, and the degree to which this is abstract and 'just gaming' in relation to the historical specificity of the drama.

NARRATIVE: As the construction of game stories is reliant on the player progressing through the programme by trial and error and by learning, we are presented with a fundamentally new, interactive form of narrative. The equivalent might be watching the first 20 minutes of a film 10 times before moving on, but this analogy won't hold due to the active nature of viewing in this case. So is game narrative linear? How are binary oppositions used to inform the player's learning? The irony is that whilst the narrative structure of a videogame text is as complex and negotiable as one can imagine, the thematics and characterisation are incredibly reductive and simple in many cases.

But this is all well and good as long as we assume that we can straightforwardly adapt, using an acronym such as this, the same concepts to a game text as to a television, film or print text. As we shall see later, David Gauntlett (2007) argues that Media teachers should be moving away from this textual approach. He thinks that new interactive media 'break the mould' and that web 2.0 must lead to Media Studies 2.0. You can decide if you agree, once we have mapped out the debate.

ARE GAMES TEXTS?

Academics wrestling with questions of how cultural meaning comes to be made tend to agree that everything is a text – you, your name, the clothes you are wearing as you read this, the way your room is set up and decorated, the last film you saw and the music you might be listening to in the background or through headphones. Everything means, everything suggests, everything signposts. As long as we can agree that everything we see, hear, read means something to us, then we can talk about contemporary cultural life being manifested in a 'textual chain'. But there are dissenting voices when it comes to thinking of games in this way.

Most of the people writing new kinds of theories for analysing games agree that the avatar is the key distinguishing element. The avatar is the visual representation / embodiment of the player, whether already designed for you or the player's creation. This is seen as fundamentally different from traditional text-viewer or text-reader dynamics. When you watch a film, you are not in it. In addition, the way that the player occupies the game space is another key shift, not only because this is different to 'external' observation of a textual world, where you observe the verisimilitude. More importantly, it is said that narrative is, if not replaced then at least displaced, by navigation. Where there tends to be less agreement is in regard to the question of how much narrative matters in this spatial experience, as Dovey and Kennedy illustrate:

> 'Contemporary mainstream console games and popular online games participate in what we might call an intermedial representational strategy. Techniques of film, graphic and text are combined in ways that reference existing forms of representation such as cinema, television, sport or literature. Mainstream games today are rich in representational pleasures that overlay and enhance the game-play mechanic. It is also evident from designers' discussions that this level of representational "realism" is highly desired and actively sought by designers and, importantly, players.' (Dovey and Kennedy, 2006: 88)

In other words, games are different from other kinds of texts because they are intermedial; but at the same time this intermedial reliance on meanings already circulated by 'older' forms of media connects game to more traditional forms of narrative and representation. In fact it is clear that many of the most popular games are ironically very new and postmodern in terms of how they look and how they are played but also incredibly old fashioned in terms of their subject matter and the situations (or maybe stories) they present to the player.

So what kinds of media language can we identify in games that we can then use to assess this debate about whether games are texts or not? Let's use the Nintendo DS game *Charlotte's Web* to explore this.

Charlotte's Web – *an intermedial text?*

Charlotte's Web is clearly intermedial as it takes as its key reference points a novel and two film versions, the more recent of which is the commercially related product to the game. Eight-year-old Lydia, who is playing the game having read the book and seen the film, here describes the game play, in relation to the book and the film:

> 'It's not like either, it's just a really good Nintendo game. Lots of the moves you can do are not in the film. You have to collect different things for each character and win levels, and get away from rats, crows and jaybirds. It is half like a story and half like a game. You can go to the storybook and there are pictures from the film with writing. And you can do things that are in the book like collect 20 gooselings for Gussy. But you don't need to read the book or see the film to play the game.'

The best way to deconstruct any media text is to construct one yourself (this goes without saying, really). But this book is primarily concerned with studying games so it isn't in our remit to spend time on design principles and technical skills. That said it is still highly productive to get a sense of how games are constructed in order to reverse the process to analyse how the elements have been put together. According to Burn and Durran (2007), when you design a game you are applying literary and semiotic principles – this is essentially language work. Using appropriate software, the designer develops a rule editor which is on the bottom of the screen unseen by the player. The rules which are inserted here correspond, in literacy terms, to what is knows as the 'conditionality clause' or the 'if-clause'. 'Game grammar' is then comprised of a combination of semiotic (a range of signs) and linguistic (conditionality – if this, then that) constructions. Later we shall see how academics have disagreed about whether games are 'narratological' or 'ludic' but Burn and Durran see the two as co-existent:

> 'The whole point of conditionality in a game, of course, is that it makes it possible for the player to play; to navigate the ludic possibilities of the game, and to participate in the narrative possibilities.' (Burn and Durran, 2007: 121)

In *Charlotte's Web*, conditionality works on many levels. Most simply, as with any game, the player learns (either through trial and error or perusal of the instruction booklet) the kinds of things Lydia describes here:

> 'With Wilbur the pig you can press A once and he will jump and if you press A twice he will double jump. If you press R with Templeton he will run.'

In addition, the player can access map screens that reveal an exit arrow. The most important condition is that passing an exit arrow allows you to complete a level. Touching a power-up icon with the DS stylus pen adds the power up to the number shown on screen and thus stored at the player's disposal. Clearly these are mundane observations, all videogames are overflowing with such 'if, then' clauses. But to deconstruct the game at the level of design, this is the rule economy at work, and we must come to an understanding of this in equal measure to our analysis of the story, themes and representations.

Conditionality functions, in technical terms, by the insertion of a 'trigger' which is a simple act of programming that physically renders the conditionality rule desired – if an avatar touches this object or space, then this triggers an action. Alongside triggers, the designer will develop a more or less complex 'rule economy' to enable the player to work within set quantities of criteria – in *Charlotte's Web* these are strength, number of lives, items collected which are of different uses at different times, power-ups to collect, letters to collect and food. A key aspect of the rule economy in this game is learning which power-ups can be used by which characters. This element of game play often alienates uninitiated adults – trial and error memory acquisition can be frustrating. For example, the instruction manual explains:

> 'Bucking Bronco: this Power-Up allows Wilbur to kick like a Bucking Bronco and lets him kick his way past troublesome critters. This Power-Up is only for Wilbur.' (SEGA, 2006: 12)

So we can say that videogames are made up of complex intermedial / multimodal (combining a variety of other media forms together) arrangements of media language. These elements are both semiotic (signs and codes) and linguistic (to do with rules and the 'game grammar'). So the player is effectively learning to read the game as well as play the game.

Lydia (aged 8) – learning conditionality

GAME GENRES

Genre is a contested concept and rather than take it for granted and apply it to videogames, it is more useful to see it as an experiment – are games generic and does their multimodal approach work to reinforce or challenge genre boundaries? A good starting point (simply because the web 2.0 nature of the information seems to fit with the 'transgressive' nature of videogames) is this list from wikipedia (accessed 5.6.07):

http://en.wikipedia.org/wiki/Video_game_genres

Contents
1 Action
1.1 Action-adventure
1.1.1 Stealth
1.1.2 Survival horror
1.2 Fighting
1.2.1 Scrolling Fighter/Brawler/Hack and Slash
1.2.2 Versus Fighter/One on One
1.3 Maze
1.4 Pinball
1.5 Platform
1.6 Shooter
1.6.1 First-person shooter
1.6.2 Light gun shooter
1.6.3 Massively multiplayer online first person shooter
1.6.4 Rail shooter
1.6.5 Run and gun
1.6.6 Shoot 'em up
1.6.7 Tactical shooter
1.6.8 Third-person shooter
1.6.9 Top-down shooter
1.7 Side-scrolling
2 Adventure
2.1 Text adventure / Interactive fiction
2.2 Graphic adventure
2.2.1 Escape the room
2.3 Visual novel
2.4 Interactive movie
3 Construction and management simulation
3.1 City-building
3.2 Economic simulation
3.3 God games
3.4 Government simulation
4 Life simulation
4.1 Biological simulation
4.2 Pet-raising simulation
4.3 Social simulation
5 Role-playing
5.1 Action role-playing
5.2 Massively multiplayer online role-playing
5.3 Roguelike
5.4 Tactical role-playing
6 Strategy
6.1 4X
6.2 Artillery
6.3 Real-time strategy
6.4 Real-time tactics
6.5 Tower Defense
6.6 Turn-based strategy
6.7 Turn-based tactics
6.8 Wargames
7 Vehicle simulation
7.1 Flight
7.2 Racing
7.3 Space
7.4 Train
7.5 Vehicular combat
8 Other notable genres
8.1 Music
8.2 Party
8.3 Programming
8.4 Puzzle
8.5 Sports
8.6 Traditional
9 Video game genres by purpose
9.1 Adult
9.2 Advergame
9.3 Casual
9.4 Christian
9.5 Educational
9.6 Exergame
9.7 Serious
9.8 Survival Horror
10 Notes
11 References
12 See also
12.1 Game interfaces
12.2 Game platforms
12.3 Other game classifications

ACTIVITY 1.1

Assuming you are working in a course group, each student brings in sufficient games for you to have at least 20 to work with. Categorise them using the genre list from Wikipedia. For each game, also answer the following questions:

• *Does it fit easily into one genre?*

• *Might it be a hybrid game (crosses generic boundaries, fits more than one)?*

• *Does it fit with genre(s) because of the playing experience or how it is marketed, or both?*

• *Does it fulfil the generic expectations in comparison to other games of this type?*

Then, in the larger group, discuss the following points:

• *How useful is genre for classifying games?*

• *How limiting is genre in reducing your gaming experiences?*

Burn and Carr (2006) here summarise the complexities of game genres, and it is likely that your discussions in response to the activity above were on similar lines:

'We could prioritise one aspect of a computer game in order to simplify or expedite its generic classification, but in truth these games are hybrid forms, and thus they invite compound classifications. Computer games are played on various platforms; they incorporate different rules, outcomes and obstacles and they represent their worlds, themes and inhabitants in different ways. Generic classification that foregrounds any one of these factors would be valid, yet, taken in isolation, each would be (to varying degrees) partial. Thus, a game can simultaneously be classified according to the platform on which it is played (PC, mobile phone, XBox), the style of play it affords (multiplayer, networked, or single user, for instance), the manner in which it positions the player in relation to the game world (first person, third person, 'god'), the kind of rules and goals that make up its game play (racing game, action adventure) or its representational aspects (science fiction, high fantasy, urban realism).' (Burn and Carr, 2006: 16)

This is a helpful description and you might productively return to the Wikipedia list and assess its value with Burn and Carr's challenges in mind. But there is one problem with this statement, which is the idea that a generic analysis which only looks at, say, themes alone (which might be more of a literary approach) would be limited but still valid. In fact, it would be not only invalid but also profoundly skew our academic understanding of videogames towards a form of analysis normally found in English literature. This is not just a pedantic point, it is of real importance. If the unique nature of videogames is to be theorised appropriately by Media students it is essential that simplistic genre labelling is at least questioned.

On the other hand, Burn and Carr are correct to remind us that genre is a huge part of the gaming experience, from the marketing of games to the ways in which reviews, websites and fan sites are organised. If we are looking for a media form that demonstrates the reductive 'contract' of genre then we need look no further than games, despite their (post)modernity. Players do not look beyond genre categorisation in most cases, despite the fluidity and hybrid nature of the games they are playing.

GAME NARRATIVES

As we shall see, there is a big debate over whether games are narratives that you play or games that have stories. In many ways it depends on the game – does *Ape Academy* have a narrative in the same way as *The Godfather*? Clearly not. But some argue that even *The Godfather*, despite its dependency on the film story, is not really a narrative form in the 'normal' sense, simply because the player interacts and effectively 'writes' the action. Let's use these two examples to tease about these issues. Those that wish to apply classic narrative theory to games do so because they believe that games have basic stories that are clearly linked to classic myths, fables and 'handed down' story themes. However, this tends to work better if you limit your analysis to certain games and ignore others. Playing *The Godfather*, an understanding of the film narrative is not required but it is possible that this provides more pleasure – the chance to 'be' the film's main protagonist affords exciting identity-play for fans of the film, it is fair to assume. The game features a host of cut scenes which are derived from the classic scenes of the film, and you are rewarded as you progress with these – you are placed more clearly in the film's world. Just as the film relies on classic character types (although the anti-hero thematic of the gangster film complicates the hero-villain binary) and a clear problem-resolution structure (the threat to the mob's power and the need for the previously innocent son to take the helm), the game uses the same conventions. But if we distinguish narrative (what we experience or see) from story (the rest of what 'happens' that we infer or assume) we can start to think about how much of the experience is derived from the film's story rather than the game's. However close at this point the game might seem to the film, and thus to narrative theory, the unique nature of 'game time' (Newman, 2004) makes this problematic. Whereas the film of *The Godfather* employs two time frames – the time it takes for the narrative to be shown (a few hours), and the story time (several years), the game doesn't share this distinction so easily. On the one hand, it is experienced always in the immediate present tense, but on the other, it can be paused, saved and returned to indefinitely. Whilst this is also true of books and DVD versions of films, the interactive nature of the 'staggered' use of the game is different. *Ape Academy* also has a narrative – you are an ape training in a military-style camp, being bullied by an authority figure and your objective is to progress though various levels to ultimately 'earn your stripes'. This, then, is a story – the story of your progress, just as any sports game also has a story of sorts, trying to win the World Cup in *Fifa 06*, for example. But it is a story with much less of a connection to theories of fictional narrative that we might use for *The Godfather*.

A 'narratologist', then, will see both games as extensions of other forms of media, as spatial stories. And although they will have an easier time with *The Godfather* than they will with *Ape Academy* due to the former being so closely related to an existing narrative from literature and film, they will also try to extend the concept of narrative to analyse the latter. But a 'ludologist' will see the simulation element of both games as fundamental. The rule systems and types played in each game will be of greater value in analysing them from this perspective. And it is probably fair to say that the ludologist will have an easier time with *The Godfather* than the narratologist will with *Ape Academy*.

Burn and Parker (2003) see videogames as using a 'narrative multimodality' which functions through a combination of interactive and non-interactive elements (the cut scenes and information to be read / heard). These are mutually dependent. Alongside this dynamic, they describe three interdependent modalities that game narratives establish – the naturalistic modality (how the bits we control blend with those we don't), the technological modality (how we come to control the game) and the sensory modality (the way we believe that we are in the game – our sense of 'flow'). However, these authors use a *Harry Potter* game to apply this model, which works very well, but is again a game which lends itself more easily to narrative theory than a host of others.

LUDOLOGY

Gonzalo Frasca here sets out a ludologist's response to the narratologists' approach outlined above:

'The storytelling model is not only an inaccurate one but also it limits our understanding of the medium and our ability to create even more compelling games. Unlike traditional media, videogames are not just based on representation but on an alternative semiotical structure known as simulation. Even if simulations and narratives do share some common elements (characters, settings and events) their mechanics are

ACTIVITY 1.2

Conduct some small scale primary research with three 7–10-year-olds (family or friends) who are currently playing a videogame that is based on an existing fictional text – a book, film or TV drama – and is intended for their age group. At the time of writing these might be *Charlotte's Web*, *Harry Potter*, *Dr Who* or *Cars*.

Ensure their parents are present. Ask each child to think about their game and, over a period of a week, to write, make or draw something that will introduce a new player to the game. Say no more than that, so you don't lead them to a particular kind of response.

When you are given their responses, in a small group compare and assess each response in regard to the following research questions:

• *What percentage of each response and the responses overall is related to the game as a story (plot, characters, drama)?*

• *What percentage of each response and the responses overall is related to the game as a game (rules, strategies, skills)?*

Your findings here will help you make up your own mind about the narrative / ludology debate.

essentially different.' (Frasca, in Wolf and Perron [eds], 2003: 221-2)

Here is one we prepared earlier. This is a slightly different exercise, as the respondent was playing *Nintendogs* rather than a game based on fiction, but it still reveals some interesting findings in relation to ludology. Lydia, aged 8, observing her Dad in the process of writing this book, went away voluntarily and came back with several pages of writing and drawings about *Nintendogs* (for us to include in the book, as 'information about the game', in her words).

Here is an extract, exactly as written:

'First you press the power button until the warning comes up. Then touch the screen. A menu will appear so you have to press the picture with the puppy on. The game will then start. Press the screen again when a labrodour appears. Press go out, then shopping then the kennel. Press look to see some dogs on show but not for sale. Press buy to choose a breed of dog. Once you have chosen your breed (example, labradour retreviour) click on the dog you would like. A icon like this means the dog is a boy, and the icon like this. Once you have chosen read the message telling you what the dog is like (such as the young female has a very bright personality and is highly recommended highly for first time dog owners). Then look at the price and at the bottom of the left.

The amount of money you have. When your dog is home you have to spend time with it, then you will see a screen so that you can tell the dog its name then you can type it up. You can then go everywhere with it like on walks, go to the pet supply and but treats are others second hand shop and lots of others. To get more money you have to go to contests. The contests are agility trail (jumping corse) obedience trail (tricks) and disk competitions (fetching and training). You can only have 3 contests a day with each dog and need to train them to do it! Have fun with your dogs!'

If you are a product of the literacy elements of the English National Curriculum then you will be familiar with the distinctions made between fictional and informative writing, formality and informality. Lydia is very much immersed in these classifications, being an enthusiastic reader and writer. What is highly significant for our work here is this – she has instinctively decided that the most appropriate 'mode of address' for writing about *Nintendogs* is informal and informational. This was fairly obvious. But look again at her writing and think about the claims made by games analysts who understand games fundamentally as narratives, as literary. There is very little in Lydia's ideas to suggest that she understands *Nintendogs* as a *story*. Her writing observes the conventions of an instruction manual. So far we can definitely decide on one thing – if narratology does work for videogames, then it won't work for these kinds of simulation games. Your research exercise, explained above, can take us a step further. Will the kids you talk to decide to write / draw / make a 'literary' response to the game or something along the same lines as Lydia?

Games analysts who prefer to see games as games, rather than games as stories, argue that it just isn't good enough to adapt narrative theory to this new form of text, or even to assume that these games *are* texts. Espen J. Aarseth argues that the narrative elements of games are certainly there for us to identity (particularly in games like *Charlotte's Web* or *The Godfather* where the player takes on an established character) but they aren't very important, indeed the player may not take much notice of them. Instead writers like Aarseth prefer an approach called 'ludology' (studying the act of play) and this way of reading games pays particular attention to the structure of play, and the degree to which games share structures. The big debate is this: 'Narratologists' think games share narrative principles with older forms of media like film and TV and even older ones like novels, and therefore being media literate means applying conceptual principles like narrative to all these kinds of text, including games. But ludologists argue that this misses the point that the game player is doing something fundamentally different to the film viewer or novel reader. She is playing, not just watching or reading, so our analysis must begin with this distinction. Moreover, she is controlling the flow of game time, whereas a TV viewer, even with live pause technology, is constrained by pre-ordained editorial decisions. Dovey and Kennedy summarise some of these textual differences here:

'Meaning generated by play is different to meaning generated by reading. To read is to create meaning cognitively in the encounter with the text. To play is to generate meaning, to express it through play. Play allows us to actively express meaning (to be part of your clan, to be a stealth assassin or princess rescuing plumber). By playing out these roles we are temporarily inhabiting an avatar that functions as part of the gameplay and offers consumers a point of entry in to the game world. Because we know we are going to be using our characters and their world for purposes other than pure interpretive pleasure, we have far less investment or interest in the meanings generated by the worlds we inhabit. This is not to argue that representation and meaning are not in play. Players clearly have interpretive responses to game worlds, and computer games in their wider circulation are clearly meaningful. However, the importance of player's interpretive pleasure is less than it would be in a novel or film.' (Dovey and Kennedy, 2006: 102)

HOW DO GAMES REPRESENT?

Representation is the most important and least contestable of all the key media concepts. Whilst we might argue about whether genre is really a useful way of categorising texts, whether games are really narratives or whether media audience theory is outdated in the wake of web 2.0 and 'DIY media', it is hard to argue with the idea that media texts of all kinds play an important role in representing people, events and ideas, and that the reader of a media text plays an active role in constructing these representations through their own cultural and life situation.

Toland (2004) suggests that games position and situate us to accept, in many cases, old fashioned and simplistic representations of gender and ethnicity. For example, in *Grand Theft Auto*, Chinese characters tend to be gangsters. Brey *et al* (1998) developed a 'semiotic' approach to game representation, by looking at the oppositions and relationships between elements and characters that add up to a coherent system of meaning in the game. Some of the questions you ask of a game with this approach are – who has the most agency (ability to influence), who is absent from the game (e.g. women or the disabled), who is active and passive in certain situations, which characters have a voice and which are silent, and what roles are allocated to which characters? Toland shows us that games have two levels when understood through this semiotic theory – on the one hand, it's 'just a game' but on the other it reinforces a range of representational codes:

'At one level the game is recreational and escapist, at another, its depiction of winners and losers sends out a broader social signal – "win" and "lose" carry connotations or "right" and "wrong".' (Toland, 2004: 18)

A major feature of some popular games which might seem to connect them (make them intermedial) to books and films in particular is the notion of threat and the construction of 'the other'. A range of games feed on the established themes of science fiction, in many cases being 'spin-offs' of films. But others establish their own game worlds where

ACTIVITY 1.3

A common way of approaching videogames as representational is to compare how different games portray a theme or situation, such as conflict or competition or gender, crime or ethnicity.

Choose three games that all share the same theme or depict a similar 'world' or time period. Play each game and in a group set up a blog or wiki to share – with hyperlinks to game play sequences where possible – ideas about how the games compare in the ways they do the following:

- *Offer an easily recognisable set of locations and situations that the player can identify.*

- *Use stereotypes.*

- *Create simple ideas about good and bad, winning and losing.*

- *Provide an experience which might exclude some people or make them feel uncomfortable.*

- *Relate to existing media texts (being intermedial or multimodal).*

- *Have some kind of a message.*

How easy was it to agree on the forum about these questions? The easier the debate, then the more straightforward the games' representations. We can use a theory from Mikhael Bakhtin to distinguish between a monoglot text (with one central set of ideas that the player really has to believe to get through the game) and a heteroglot text (where there are a number of different 'world views' to choose from in understanding the text). Do the games seem monoglot or heteroglot?

But here is where it gets complicated and we return to the 'old chestnut' about whether our media concepts are robust enough for this challenge. Whereas it is likely that someone with particular views will not spend time watching TV or films that totally conflict with them, is it somehow easier to play a game that has an ideology you don't like? If so, this seems strange because you might expect to be more upset by the experience of being immersed in a world that has a morality that conflicts with your own. But for some reason, many players report being able to play a particularly violent game or a game with an extreme capitalist ethos which distorts their own 'ideological compass' but feel more comfortable doing this than watching a film with a similar world view precisely because the game feels less representative of the 'real world', or appears to be less active in constructing representations of this kind. Put far more simply, it's 'only a game' after all. Discuss.

civilisation is threatened by an enemy. The emerging range of game design software available to Media students, some of which you may have worked with, tend to take this construction of heroes and – more importantly – villains as a starting point, and for this reason English teachers can find ways of using games in relation to more established forms of literacy. Burn and Durran (2007) call this 'game literacy' and suggest that it is not only possible but also useful to use the theories of narrative established many years ago by Vladimir Propp (who was analysing Russian folk tales) to analyse characters, stories and themes in modern games. Propp's famous theory (1968) tells us that most stories in Western culture share a limited range of character types, and Burn and Durran explain that this hasn't really changed despite all the technological and cultural shifts that have happened since Propp was writing. So what links games to folk tales, books, plays, films, TV drama and a whole range of other forms (again, what makes them intermedial) is the way that being literate enough to play them demands an understanding of character types:

> 'Propp analysed the narrative structures of Russian folk tales and discovered a high degree of conformity to a limited number of narrative patterns. These included the narrative functions of certain recurrent character types, such as a hero, a false hero, a villain, donor, a princess, a father figure, a helper, a dispatcher. Propp's approach suits the formulaic nature of computer game narratives which resembles folk tales and oral formulaic stories more generally. This is partly because they often draw on ancient narrative forms (quest narratives, sagas, romances, epics). It is relatively easy for students to imagine Propp's character types in ways which fit the episodic structure of games, and the rewards, challenges, obstacles and so on which also form part of the game structure.' (Burn and Durran, 2007: 114-15)

This is true and useful as long as we are clear that there are more games that don't fit this model than those that do. As long as we are limiting our analysis to more 'literary' games with fictional characters, then applying Propp will help us to work at this intermedial level well. But if we are studying a tennis game or *SingStar* it won't get us anywhere. This is why it is so important to set out the terms of your analysis when dealing with games – what types of game are you talking about, specifically?

But we are not for a moment suggesting that playing a tennis game does not involve an understanding of representation – just that the way it is mediated is fundamentally different. The *mise-en-scène* is important so that the player feels like they are really playing tennis in a tournament. It may be possible to select different courts. The player may have a choice over which real famous tennis player they want to be. The on-screen player / avatar may be pre-designed and chosen or created by the player. There will be ideological features in this – the reinforcing of visual codes about physical shape, possible branding and ethnic representations will be there to analyse. For games like *SingStar* there is gender representation to consider. Clearly this kind of game has played an important role in bringing more females to the games market. But there are issues here about the polarised nature of game marketing – the games industry is not very progressive when it

ACTIVITY 1.4

There are five important gender questions to ask about any game, which are the following:

• *Is the game representing one gender as more active than the other?*

• *In what range of ways does it represent the active gender to itself?*

• *In what range of ways does it represent the active gender to the other gender?*

• *In what range of ways does it represent the passive or less active gender to itself?*

• *In what range of ways does it represent the passive or less active gender to the other gender?*

Taking one game which you consider to be targeted at one gender much more than the other, answer the above questions, and then use this research as the starting point for a pitch for a new game of your invention which reverses the gender representation at work in the 'real' game. If what you produce seems absurd (or at least commercially unviable) then what does this tell us about representation in videogames?

comes to creating audiences, as Newman and Oram illustrate:

'Over the last decade, as it has attempted to expand its market and sell more games to more people, the videogame industry has become increasingly interested in women gamers. This may have less to do with righting the apparent wrongs of previous eras and more to do with economic opportunity but, nonetheless a number of strategies have emerged…(But) critics point to the potentially "ghettoising" nature of "games for girls". In a retail environment, the (usually small) "games for girls" section might be seen to serve as an indication that everything else is "not for girls". (Newman and Oram, 2006: 72)

Many academics also think we should move away from seeing games as stories because the intermedial effect doesn't only connect certain games to pre-existing stories, it also drastically changes the ways that meanings get made. This happens when the game is surrounded by an array of networking – from online cheat guides to player forums to the distribution of 'patches' to fan sites and to fan art and fan writing, as Burn describes:

'Engagement with the game does not finish when the game session ends and the computer or console is switched off. Players continue to think about, imagine, even dream about, the events, landscapes and characters of the game; and particularly committed fans go further, joining online communities of fans and contributing to message boards, art galleries, writing groups and other forms of expansive embroidery of the game and its components.' (Burn, in Carr et al, 2006: 88)

When we add social play – people connecting online to play games or to take part in virtual lives, as in the case of the emerging range of Massively Multiplayer Online

Role Playing Games (MMORPG) – to the mix, we move even further away from the traditional character, story, reader relations that we know from books. But representation is just as crucial – perhaps even more so – as the player constructs an idealised representation of her / himself through which to connect to strangers online, described by Rehak (2003) as 'playing at being'. Rehak offers a very interesting but very complex analysis of how players design avatars using psychoanalytical theory, mostly derived from Lacan, and it is not terribly helpful to go into lots of detail here (for more on psychoanalysis and Lacan, see McDougall and Peim, 2007). But the really important point Rehak makes is this – firstly, the avatar merges spectatorship with participation and this is completely new in the history of media, and secondly, what the videogame does is make explicit the pleasure and pain of being in the world as a subject and object simultaneously – precisely the situation Freud, Lacan and other psychoanalysts have been writing about for decades! In simpler terms, from a very young age (described by Lacan as the 'mirror stage' [1979]) we come to realise that we exist as subject to ourselves and object to others. Subsequently, every moment of our lives is spent with this understanding in mind. How we want to behave is not the same as how we want to be viewed. Debates about the television programme *Big Brother*, the increase in CCTV since 9/11 and the increase in mobile phone camera and video use all relate to this psychological issue. And Rehak suggests that the construction of an avatar in a videogame or MMORPG takes us back to the 'mirror stage' in a way that a film, TV programme or novel can't:

> 'We create avatars to leave our bodies behind, yet take the body with us in the form of codes and assumptions about what does and does not constitute a legitimate interface with reality – virtual or otherwise.' (Rehak, in Wolf and Perron [eds], 2003: 123)

GAME LITERACY

The popular myth, as we established in the introduction, is that videogames are contributing to a 'dumbed down', passive, antisocial and less literate generation of children than in previous non-digital eras. And, of course, this is nonsense. Indeed, as Johnson (2005) argues, a more intelligent observation would be to bear witness to ways in which games and other new media forms are 'making us sharper'. At an obvious level, it is clear that there is a wide range of literature surrounding games which means that many gamers also read written material about games whether in magazines, on websites or novels that games are based on (see Marsh and Millard, 2000 and Kendall, 2008). But to consider literacy development within game playing itself, we must turn to James Paul Gee (2003), an academic who has gone out of his way to prove this, producing a book titled *What Videogames Have to Teach us About Learning and Literacy*. We discuss the ways that games develop literacy in detail in the chapter on social effects, but it is worth spending a little time on this here also as it does impact on how we use media concepts with games. A traditional approach is to consider media language in games, and as we have discussed, this will be a fusion of various elements of media language derived from film, popular music and other sources – the intermedial / multimodal effect. But if, as Gee suggests, learning a game is essentially a process of language acquisition then this goes beyond media language and takes us to a place where teachers know less than students about the language to be studied, a situation Kendall (2008) describes as 'the pedagogy of the inexpert'. How can we assess this idea that 'new literacies' are manifested in game playing? One way of describing this is to think about the way young people use multimedia / intermedial sources as a matter of course (in a way that older people find threatening and alienating) as 'remixing' (Lankshear and Knobel, 2006).

VIDEOGAMES AS POSTMODERN MEDIA

At least one of the major awarding bodies in the UK invites Media students to analyse videogames and other new media forms under the heading 'postmodern'. Put simply, those of the 'postmodern persuasion' (Masterman, 2006) are of the view that in our media-saturated world it is no longer as clear as it used to be how reality and media representations of reality are distinct from one another. The videogame, for these people, would seem to be an ideal example of this blurring. This state of uncertainty over these boundaries was described by the French philosopher Jean Baudrillard (1988) as 'hyper-reality'. Two useful concepts to help us with this approach are **flow** and **immersion**. Psychological immersion (as opposed to perceptual) is our focus here, the way in which a player invests her imagination in the game and is thus absorbed into the game's world, even with a small screen like the DS or PSP. Csikszentmihályi (1996) describes that state of flow as that in which an activity demands ever increasing, but highly pleasurable and achievable challenges and offers constant feedback on levels of progress.

> 'It is easy to recognise the conditions of flow. These include having a clear goal or problem to solve, ability to discern how well one is doing, struggling forward in the face of challenges until the creative process begins to hum and one is lost in the task, and enjoying the activity for its own sake.' (Csikszentmihályi, 1996: 113)

This might take us off on a tangent – why do the same kids (you might be one) who get criticised by their teachers for demonstrating no intrinsic motivation at school spend so much time playing videogames which are certainly challenges for their own sake? But to return to our theme of the postmodern nature of videogames, flow is interesting because it describes a state whereby immersion (the pleasurable loss of reality) becomes hard work, but creative and pleasurable at the same time. Being 'lost' in the game, it seems, leads to an enhanced state of pleasure that is entirely dependent on the *hyper-real* nature of the experience.

ACTIVITY 1.5

Choose a person you know to be a non-videogamer. Give them a game of your choice, the instruction booklet and game, and observe them for one hour as they start making their way through the game. When they ask for help, give it. As you observe and intervene, make some notes on their level of game literacy. In what ways are they illiterate? What forms of literacy do they develop in this hour? What potential do they have to become fully game-literate over time?

GAME AUDIENCES AND MEDIA STUDIES 2.0

In the chapter on the social effects of videogames, we explore in detail the various theories of how players are constructed into game audiences and how researchers wrestle with their responses. But we must first be aware of the argument that videogames present a threat to traditional notions of media audiences. Whilst it is clear that the industry use some pretty old fashioned notions of audience, particularly on gender lines, to promote and distribute games, some academics argue that the nature of game audiences cannot be explained by the 'traditional' Media Studies approach. Dovey and Kennedy suggest that Media Studies has tended to look at *active audiences*, meaning it is concerned with the dynamic, varied ways in which audiences make sense of media texts, and they assert that videogames are best understood by shifting this approach to an analysis of *interactive* users. Gauntlett (2007) agrees, going further to suggest a new approach – Media Studies 2.0. This approach starts from the premise (which may sound odd) that Media Studies is sometimes too much *about* the media, and not enough about *people using the media* alongside other aspects of cultural life to construct identities. The simplest way to describe this is to say that Media Studies 2.0 will be concerned with individuals using videogames, other media forms and interactive networks to construct social and cultural identities. This doesn't work if we group individuals together into audience groups and then make assumptions about shared responses to games. What it means for you is this – a really good analytical response to videogames will require you to carry out research with individuals, asking questions about the way their individual identity connects to the game cultures they inhabit. Central to this is the notion of play – if we study games most rigorously as games rather than try to see them as stories we interact with, this can help us understand more fully the playful nature of identity construction in our new media culture:

'The Media Studies literature on audiences has a tendency to acknowledge the diversity of audiences – that an audience may be comprised of a range of different people with different interests and backgrounds – but then proceeds anyway, as if talking about "audiences" is fine as long as you mention this first. In fact, of course, it is the case that audiences are not only a diverse set of individuals but that each individual is complex, internally diverse and often somewhat contradictory in attitudes, tastes and pleasures. The media engages with these interests, and makes a substantial contribution to satisfying them.' (Gauntlett, 2007: 193)

So how can you apply this new kind of approach? How can you study videogames from a Media Studies 2.0 perspective? This activity might seem completely bizarre at first, but give it a go. It is derived from Gauntlett's own approach to audience research and identity analysis. Gauntlett has developed a research method for exploring how people construct identities using Lego. This method asks research participants to make metaphorical models with Lego to represent their identities and then to discuss how they came to represent themselves metaphorically in these ways (for a fuller understanding of how the Lego research method works, see Chapter 8 of his *Creative Explorations*). He describes the metaphorical approach in this way:

'A participant would typically pick up certain parts from the Lego boxes without really knowing at that point how they were going to come together to have metaphorical meaning – but then meanings would soon emerge when the building began. For example, a person might choose a tiger to represent pride and assertiveness, and then put the tiger on wheels to give it movement; but then would realise that the wheels could not be steered, so that the proud tiger tended to race forwards and crash into things; and then this characteristic became incorporated into the "official" meaning of the model, because the person recognised that this was a good representation of her character. Metaphors would often appear "by accident" in this way.' (Gauntlett, 2007: 184)

WHEN LIFE IS A GAME

At the time of writing, *Second Life* is big news. *Second Life* is a virtual world which anyone can live in through a broadband connection, by creating an avatar and moving around Linden Island, interacting with the thousands of other avatars. It is possible to do pretty much anything virtually on the island, from watching a 'real' movie or a band performing to less wholesome activities. A 3D online world, *Second Life* has attracted 'residents' from over 100 countries. Very much part of the 'peer authored' web 2.0, the distinguishing feature of *Second Life* is the way that the virtual residents themselves create and build the world, designing and paying for land and then homes, vehicles, shops, clothing and games. A rapidly increasing number of colleges and universities are setting up virtual campuses on the island and facilitating student learning through avatar seminars and lectures. There are even conferences taking place entirely through *Second Life*. And there has been a range of political campaigns and demonstrations organised on the island. We have included *Second Life* in this book because we think you should study it and ask the question – is it a game? It clearly is in the sense that it uses the conventions of the simulation game and when you first enter the island it feels and looks very much like a game world. But for some commentators, like Jacquie Bennett (2007), that is where the similarity ends:

ACTIVITY 1.6

In a group of five, each conducts this experiment with one videogame player, but ensure that the group members are all keen players of the same game.

Give the player a set of Lego and ask them to construct a metaphorical model of themselves in ordinary, real life, with the Lego. This model should visually represent how they see their own everyday identity.

Next, ask them to build a metaphorical model of how they see themselves when immersed in the flow of the videogame.

Finally, record a discussion with the player, in which they reflect on the models they have built and how they are different.

Get back into your group of five, compare recordings (and photographs of the models if the players give you permission for this) and if Gauntlett is right, you will have a pretty sophisticated audience study at your disposal which will help you understand the complexity of videogame play in relation to identity construction at the level of the individual – this is the crucial bit. Good luck!

'With all video games there is a defined "objective" and for video games as opposed to multi-user online games a narrative as well. A user must "do" within this environment and has specific goals to achieve at all stages (kill this dragon and find this treasure) and receives feedback and rewards when each goal is achieved. These users often feel initially disenfranchised when they enter the *Second Life* world because they are not immediately greeted with a narrative and set a goal or task. They find the concept that they can simply "be" in this environment rather than "do" alien and sometimes intimidating.' (Bennett, 2007: 6)

And yet, despite the clarity of Bennett's distinction, if we return to Rehak's notion of 'playing at being', then *Second Life* would appear to be a very good example of this 'mirror stage' identity play which is certainly shared with videogames. The question is whether playing at being becomes being (if there is really a distinction in the first place) when there is no defined objective, as Bennett puts it.

The diagrams that follow attempt to represent visually the development of collaborative and cumulative online play.

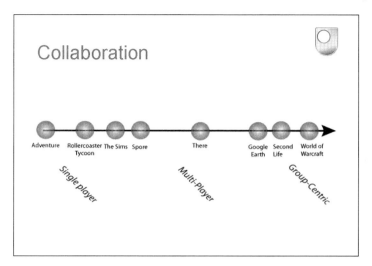

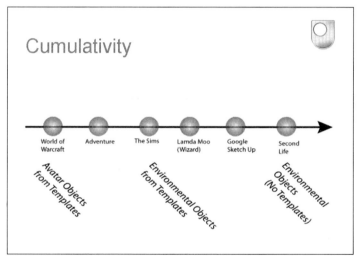

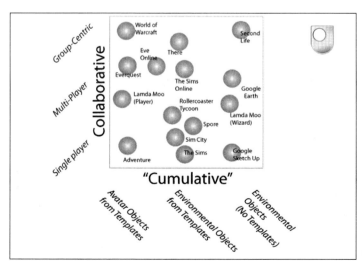

(Source: Jeremy Kemp, San Jose State University & Jacquie Bennett, Open University, used with permission)

Alongside *Second Life*, we must consider *Club Penguin*, a children's MMORPG in which the player designs their own penguin avatar and joins a community. Like Linden Island, this virtual world can be played at many levels, from simple interaction to the building of homes and the acquisition of various possessions. As this *Chicago Tribune* report suggests, the desire to be virtually successful is a feature of this 'game':

'At one increasingly popular site where young kids inhabit a fantasy world of penguins and igloos, some are downloading illicit software to stuff their virtual pockets with gold coins instead of earning their way fairly by playing games. Across the internet, blogs, message boards and even video clips on YouTube.com offer preteens tips and tricks on how to steal coins at ClubPenguin.com or cheat their way to a higher salary at Whyville.net. A simple Google search pops up hundreds of places to find such insights. Over the last three months, cheating has become such a concern at *Club Penguin* that on Tuesday the Canadian company approved new guidelines banning the practice, said Lane Merrifield, co-founder and chief executive. "If anyone is caught trying to instruct other players or is teaching them how to cheat on *Club Penguin*, even on another Web site, blog or forum, we are instituting a permanent ban on the player who is doing the teaching," he said. Parents are generally happy with sites like *Club Penguin* and *Whyville*, where their kids can play safely online and interact with other youngsters. But to some educators, the cheating is yet another example of a competitive culture looking for shortcuts to get ahead. Worse, these cheaters can be as young as 8, and by unfairly learning how to obtain the biggest igloo on the block, it could foreshadow cheating in other aspects of life, they say.' (Benderoff, 2007 at http://www.chicagotribune.com/business/chi-0703080167mar08,0,4256114.story?coll=chi-bizfront-hed, accessed 8.6.07)

As with all 'moral panics', the *Tribune* article is overstating the negative actions of a minority and of course the majority of children playing the game do so by the rules. But even then, there is a debate to be had over the psychology of 'virtual cheating' and its relationship to what we might call 'intermedial initiative'. Is it necessarily the case that 8-year-old *Club Penguin* cheats will break the rules in 'real' society?

As stated earlier, a book like this is always constrained by the time between writing and publication, so all we can do here is touch upon a 'breaking news' development that, by the time you read this, may well be old-hat. A key moment in the history of media convergence (technologies and media companies coming together) may well be the alliance of Electronic Arts and Endemol to develop *Virtual Me*, described in a press release from EA here:

Virtual Me combines cutting edge avatar creation technology from EA with popular TV formats from Endemol to give consumers a breakthrough way to meet, compete and socialize in online digital worlds. *Virtual Me* offers players the chance to participate in virtual versions of TV talent shows like *Fame Academy*, game shows like *Deal or No Deal* and to form real relationships with other virtual avatars.' (EA press release, 16.4.7)

SUMMARY

In this chapter, we have navigated our way through a range of conceptual debates and what should be clear by now is that nothing is for certain when it comes to analysing videogames. The best approach for you to take is to apply the key concepts to a range of different games and along the way do two things – deconstruct the game as a semiotic, multimodal and literary text as far as it is possible to do so, but also analyse it as a phenomena of flow, immersion and engagement – as an experienced gamer, as a ludologist. This may, or may not, lead you to at least question or even reject some of the academic concepts we have introduced here.

2. THE VIDEOGAME INDUSTRY: *SPLITTING TIME* – FROM THE PAST TO THE PRESENT TO *FUTURE PERFECT*

INTRODUCTION

Elsewhere in this book, the four key concepts of Media Studies are examined and applied to how they can be used in the study of videogames. You should see this chapter partly as a snapshot history of the industry and partly as a case study in the interactions between media audiences and media institutions. The tasks offered will require you to focus on how audiences and institutions have acted and reacted to changes within this industry.

The purpose of this chapter is to provide the reader with a broad knowledge of the history of the videogame industry – this will be achieved through going back to the roots of the sizeable 'boss' that the videogame industry has become and tracing through the major developments and twists and turns that have befallen the industry in the 35 years since the launch of the first publicly available game console. This chapter will bring the reader up to the present day and present generation of games and game consoles (as of the time of writing). Thus, to borrow the conceit from the *TimeSplitters* game series, this chapter will split time into different pieces, and go backwards and forwards through time to get back to the future, and, with the help of some experts from within the videogame industry, will investigate the possible permutations of the future directions the videogame industry may go. The videogame industry (comprising game consoles, PC gaming, handheld gaming and arcade gaming) is now a very big one – too large to meaningfully do justice to all sectors of the industry in one chapter. Therefore, the focus of this chapter is the consoles sector of the videogame industry as this is the major player within the sector as a whole. For further information on the other sectors of the videogame industry, there is some recommended reading at the end of the chapter.

In the years since the launch of 64-bit consoles such as Sony's PlayStation (now known as the PS1) and Nintendo's N64, amongst other consoles, the videogame industry has mushroomed in terms of the volume of money flowing through it and its public profile. The public profile of the industry has mostly been a troublesome one – with regular moral panics engineered by reactionary forces in society and the media about a number of videogames through the years. There is much more to be said and to be known about videogames and the videogame industry than just the small handful of games which attract negative publicity. This chapter breaks the history of the industry into three separate sections – the past, the present and the future.

'The past' details the birth of the industry and growing pains felt since its inception. The first section travels through time from 1972 and the launch of the first publicly available game console, Magnavox's Odyssey to 2005 and Microsoft's XBox and takes in all points in between. The second section on 'the present' takes the reader from the launch of the PlayStation 2 (hereafter referred to as the PS2) in 2000 up to the launch of the PS3 in 2007. The final section on 'the future' focuses on the possible directions the industry might take and explores some of the issues which face, or may face, the industry in the future.

THE KEY EVENTS OF THE VIDEOGAME INDUSTRY

In order to make a complicated history more accessible a timeline of the key events within the videogame industry is documented below. This focuses on industry events rather than on game releases for the sake of brevity and clarity. For details on release of landmark games, see *Edge*, special edition, 'The 100 Best Videogames' (*Edge presents...* I, Future Publishing, 2007).

Time	Action
1958	William Higinbotham and Robert Dvorak develop the first electronic interactive game – *Tennis For Two* – only available for play in a laboratory, using technology developed for analysing missile trajectories.
1961	*Spacewar!* is developed for the purposes of demonstrating the capacity of mainframe computers. This was available for play by students at a number of universities – a strictly limited version for the public.
September 1972	Magnavox's Odyssey – part games console and part board game – is launched. Priced at $100, it sold 100,000 units in the USA. The era of the games console had arrived.
1972	Atari is founded – this company would be one of the major players in the industry over the course of the 70s and 80s.
1973	Atari makes $3.2m from sales of arcade units for its *Pong* game – this marks the start of the boom of videogames in arcades.
1975	*Pong* comes home. Atari produces a version for the home market, thus starting the lucrative business of arcade conversions which fuelled the industry through the 70s and 80s.
1976	Warner Communication buys Atari for $28m – videogames was now an industry like any other.
1977	The Atari 2600 is launched. By 1982, 25 million 2600s are sold, earning $5bn for Atari. This initiates the first 'platform war' with the Odyssey.
1980	Mattel launches the Intellivision, which is graphically superior to the Atari 2600, selling one million units by 1983.

Time	Action
1982	Phenomenally successful arcade game *Pac-Man* is converted for the 2600. The job is done poorly; the game was an inferior copy. Atari buys the rights to produce a game of the film *E.T.*, paying $21m and manufacturing 5 million cartridges. This rushed, poor game sells 1 million copies which sparks the downturn, or crash, in the American videogame market.
1982	Commodore launches the Commodore 64, known as the C64. The success of the C64 enables Commodore to eclipse Atari as the 'boss' of the videogame industry in the early to mid 80s.
1982	The Sinclair ZX Spectrum is launched in the UK creating another round of 'platform wars'. The debate about what was best – C64 or Spectrum (or 'Speccy' as it was fondly known) – was had in many neighbourhoods and school playgrounds.
1983	In Japan, Nintendo launches the Famicom. Priced at the equivalent of $100, it sells 500,000 units in two months. Outside of Japan, the Famicom is marketed as the Nintendo Entertainment System (NES). While successful in the USA, it has limited impact in Europe due to the dominance of the C64 and the 'Speccy'.
1984	Atari has become yesterday's man – knocked sideways by the success of the C64. The Atari star begins its descent, but not without a fight in the shape of the launch of the Atari ST.
1985	Sega launches the Sega Master System (SMS). This does not fair well, due to the dominance now achieved by Nintendo – a cautionary tale lies here about being late to market.
1987	Commodore launches the Amiga A500. This picks up C64 owners looking to trade up and sees off the competition from Atari.
1989	Nintendo launches the Game Boy, achieving dominance in the handheld gaming market they have never relinquished.
1989	Sega launches the Mega Drive (marketed as the Genesis in the USA). In 1990, the MD became the most in-demand console. The MD marks Sega's high point as a console manufacturer.
1990	SNK launches the Neo-Geo, boasting graphics capability superior to its rivals, but also a higher price.
1991	Sony working in conjunction with Nintendo produces what was to become the Nintendo PlayStation. Subsequent disputes between the two companies lead to Sony's entry into the console market.
1995	The Sony PlayStation is launched, taking on and outperforming Sega's new console, the Saturn.

Time	Action
1996	Nintendo strikes back with the launch of the N64 – but the PS was cheaper, and consequently outperformed sales of the N64. Sony was here to stay.
1998	Sega launches the Dreamcast – online gaming comes to console, previously only the territory of PC gaming.
1999 / 2000	Nintendo is boosted by the overwhelming success of *Pokémon*.
2000	Sony launches the PS2 – graphically as good as the Dreamcast, but also armed with a DVD player. Convergence of technologies proved to be a winning formula.
2001	Sega announces withdrawal from the console development market. Microsoft announces its entry and the launch of the XBox.
2001	Nintendo launches the Game Cube – price positioned in the market as a budget rival to PS2 and XBox.
2001	*Grand Theft Auto 3* is released, a landmark game in the series and for the PS2 (see Chapter 4 for further details).
2004	Nintendo's latest handheld offering, the DS (for Dual Screen), is launched, beating Sony's PlayStation Portable (PSP) to market, which arrived in 2005.
2005	Nintendo launches the Wii and Microsoft launch XBox 360. The launch of Sony's PS3 is delayed allowing Microsoft a free run at the lucrative Christmas market.
2006	Sony announces the end of the manufacture of PS1. In March the PS achieves total sales of 103 million.
2007	After a series of delays, Sony launches the PS3.

THE GENERATIONS OF GAME CONSOLES

Generation	Key Consoles
1st generation	Magnavox Odyssey / Atari Pong / Coleco Telstar
2nd generation	Atari 2600 / Fairchild Channel F / Magnavox Odyssey 2 / Mattel Intellivision / ColecoVision
3rd generation	NES / Sega Master System / Atari 7800
4th generation	Sega Mega Drive / SNES / SNK Neo-Geo
5th generation	Sega Saturn / Sony PlayStation / Nintendo 64
6th generation	Sega Dreamcast / Sony PS2 / Nintendo GameCube / Microsoft XBox
7th generation	Microsoft XBox 360 / Sony PS3 / Nintendo Wii

(Sources: Flatley and French, 'Videogaming', London: Pocket Essentials, 2003 and at http://
en.wikipedia.org/wiki/History_of_video_games, accessed 22/5/07)

OUT OF THE PAST – IN THE BEGINNING...

It is quite possible that for as long as you can remember there has been a games
console in your house – it may have belonged to a sister or brother, or one or both
of your parents. As you have grown up it is fairly likely that you, or a sister or brother,
or friends, have had your / their own game consoles – such as the PS2, the XBox, the
Game Cube or handheld devices such as a Game Boy. For those of you who really like
playing videogames, you may now have a Wii, XBox 360 or PS3 – plus perhaps a PSP or
a Nintendo DS. Videogame culture is now unavoidable and a normal part of everyday life
for a great many people. However, things were not always like this: videogame culture was
not always a 'natural' part of everyday life, and the videogame industry and its products
were not always so prevalent. The aim of this section is to give you an understanding of
how the videogame industry has grown to be such a forceful 'boss' to be reckoned with.

Using the timeline as a reference point, this section focuses on some of the bigger issues
that have become milestones on the progression of the videogame industry from nothing
to big something.

TASK 2.1 – GENERATIONS RESEARCH

Objective – To carry out some research into what uses and pleasures older audiences for
older consoles have derived from playing videogames and to work out how similar and different
the experiences of playing on older consoles is to playing games on 6th and 7th generation
consoles. This will develop your knowledge and understanding of the videogame industry from
the audience perspective.

What to do:

- Speak to older brothers / sisters / cousins who have owned game consoles – find out
  what consoles they owned, what their favourite games were and what they like and
  disliked about playing games on that console.

- Repeat the exercise with a parent or other older relative.

- Next consider your own experiences of playing videogames and using games consoles
  – what are the similarities and differences in the types of uses and pleasures that players
  derive from playing videogames of different generations? How much or how little has
  the actual experience of playing videogames changed in the 30 years since the launch of
  the Atari 2600?

PLAYER 1 – GENESIS: THE ARRIVAL OF THE HOME GAME CONSOLE – THE ATARI VCS / 2600, AND THE RISE AND FALL OF ATARI

Like so many other innovations and advances, the origins of the videogame industry lie in a military context. As noted in the timeline, the game which is acknowledged as being the first videogame is *Tennis for Two*, which sprang from missile technology. A version of this game – *Pong* – would help to set in motion the path towards the home game console market. Atari developed *Pong* as an arcade game firstly, and its success as an arcade game induced Atari to manufacture and sell a home version of this game. The success of this venture led to the Atari 2600. Up until the launch of the 2600, videogames had been an exclusively social activity – if you wanted to play videogames, you went to dedicated arcades to play them, or if you were old enough, you might be able to play *Space Invaders* or *Zaxxon* in the local bar. Now, the most common mode of playing videogames is in the home and the success of the Atari 2600 helped to bring about the home console market. Here's why.

While the 2600 wasn't the first games console for the home market, that honour going to the Odyssey, what the 2600 did ultimately offer was the opportunity to play versions of arcade games at home – hence some of its biggest selling titles were arcade conversions such as *Space Invaders*. If arcades were difficult to get to or bars were simply beyond your reach because you were too young to go into them, with the 2600 you could have all the fun of the fair in your own living room. What the 2600 also introduced was the notion of the 'joystick' for playing games with. The joystick was a revolutionary step forward for game playing and avatar control – with preceding games such as *Pong* you had 'paddles' with wheels which this writer remembers as not being user-friendly. The Atari 2600 offered an enormous range of quality games, perhaps Activision's *Pitfall* being the greatest of all the games developed for it, and it offered ease of use. In any form of media technology, ease of use, over and above technical capability, generally tends to win out. So it was with the Atari 2600. As noted in the timeline, it went on to sell 25 million units – a very sizeable figure for a new type of product. However, compared to the sales figures for the PS1 and PS2 of around 200 million units combined (according to figures used in BBC news report http://news.bbc.co.uk/1/hi/technology/4807858.stm), this shows how the size and scale of the industry have mushroomed since the days of the 2600 in the late 70s and early 80s. With this type of success, Atari should have been built to last, in the same way that Nintendo has been a long-term player in videogames hardware and software. The success of any piece of media technology depends on the products that it is used with – games consoles are only as good ultimately as the games produced for them. The forces that set Atari on the road to success also undermined the company – the belief that arcade conversions would always earn money. Atari's crash and burn is a cautionary tale of bloated corporate egos and poor business management.

Atari developed two games in 1982 which dragged the company down and partly helped to send the American videogame industry into a tailspin which it would take the rest of the decade to recover from. One game was an arcade conversion of the legendary *Pac-Man* and the development of a game based on the film *E.T.* In both cases, the games produced were rough rush jobs which correspondingly sold poorly. These blackened the Atari brand name, which up until this point had become a by-word for quality in the videogame market and would adversely affect the company in the future, and in the short-term. In the early 80s, Atari made some poor business decisions which led to the loss of huge sums of money. With the case of the *E.T.* adaptation, Atari paid $21m for the licensing rights and produced 5 million cartridges – only 1 million sold; the remainder were dumped in a landfill site in New Mexico. The disasters with these games dragged Atari down, and over-saturation of the market with other consoles and games – such as the Intellivision, which first appeared in 1980 and the Colecovision which arrived in 1982 – the American videogame market was now in crisis. In 1983 Atari was losing $2m a day, $536m in the year. Atari was now mortally wounded – Player 1 was out.

TASK 2.2 – THE FALL OF ATARI: WHAT DID ATARI DO WRONG?

Objective – To consolidate your knowledge and understanding about why Atari became the first major corporate casualty of the videogame industry. This will develop your knowledge and understanding of the videogame industry from the institutional perspective.

What to do – Use www.google.com and run the following search 'Atari'. Read through a variety of articles and make 1 side of A4 notes addressing the question of what Atari did wrong.

PLAYER 2 – EXODUS: THE COMING OF THE HOME COMPUTER – THE COMMODORE 64

In any good game, or narrative, at the point where a character is struggling and falls by the wayside another comes along to take the strain. In this story, that character is Commodore computers. Like Atari, Commodore is now to be found in the 'Where are they now?' files. However, in the 80s and early 90s, Commodore was everywhere – no self-respecting British schoolchild in the 80s was without a Commodore 64 (C64 for short) – unless you were of the mistaken belief that the technically inferior ZX Spectrum was a better machine. Commodore was so ubiquitous that at one point it sponsored Chelsea FC. Commodore initially rose to prominence with the success of their VIC 20 home computer – which was the first home computer to sell one million units (Flatley and French, 2003: 18).

The C64 was originally marketed as a business machine for home use, but it quickly became most popular as a vehicle for playing games. The Atari 2600, and the other consoles available at the time were all cartridge-oriented consoles – readers who have played NES and SNES will be familiar with game cartridges. The C64 continued this tradition, having a cartridge slot, and a small number of cartridge games were produced for the C64. However, there were two other ways of loading games on a C64 – by tape and by floppy disk. Writing in 2007, it now seems antiquated to talk about floppy disks; but in the early and mid 80s, the time of peak popularity for the C64, floppy disks were a ludicrously expensive luxury. The vast majority of C64 gamers loaded their game by tape through a bespoke tape deck which connected to the computer. As the games got bigger and more complex, the loading times increased – this writer clearly remembers waiting for ages for games like *Green Beret*, *Beach Head*, *Combat School*, *Elite*, *Paradroid*, *Summer Games II* and *Winter Games* to load up. However, the tape format served the C64 well – tape games were substantially cheaper than cartridge and floppy disk games, and this in turn helped to drive sales of games, which in turn helped sell C64 units.

From the success of the C64, Commodore developed the C128, which never really caught hold of the public imagination. The development of the Amiga series did take hold – even though the launch of the Commodore Amiga A500 in 1987 proved a natural trading up point for C64 users who either wanted or needed to move on from the C64. In another reality, the Amiga should have reinforced Commodore's hold over the home computing market for the years to come. However, other technical developments in PC technology washed Commodore away as parts for PCs became ever more standardised and generic – there was no longer such an overwhelming need to have one type of computer again.

GAME ON – PLATFORM WARS: C64 VERSUS ZX SPECTRUM

In the timeline, it is noted that the first outbreak in the long-running saga of 'platform wars' (essentially contests between rival institutions for dominance of a sector of the videogame market) occurred in the late 70s when Atari encroached on the turf of Magnavox's Odyssey console / board game hybrid. Due to Atari's self-inflicted mortal wound, the next round of platform wars was fought between Commodore and Sinclair and their avatars in this game were to be the C64 and ZX Spectrum, respectively. Whilst the Spectrum didn't boast the kind of technical specification that the C64 did, it was always a keen competitor on price, costing significantly less than the C64. The parallel in the present era would be the price differences which currently exist between Nintendo's Wii and the XBox 360 – what you lose in graphical capability, you make up for in money saved.

While the Spectrum didn't possess the sound and graphics capabilities of the C64, games developers certainly maximised the capacity of the Spectrum, which enabled the Spectrum to sell many units – in the run-up to Christmas 1983, the Spectrum was selling 50,000 units a month (Retro Gamer Collection, Vol1. Imagine Publishing, 2007). In Commodore's favour was a healthier global position – the Speccy was strong in Europe and particularly the UK, but the Commodore was also strong in its home market – the USA. The staying power of the C64 is demonstrated through the fact that games are still produced for the C64 – albeit these can't be bought in the shops, but between small-scale online traders. The C64 and the Speccy still live on today through downloadable emulators and through second-hand trading of the computers.

TASK 2.3 – PLAYING GAMES, 80S STYLE

Objective – To gather first-hand knowledge of the experience of playing videogames in the 1980s on some of the major consoles / computers of the era. This will develop your knowledge and understanding of the videogame industry from the audience perspective.

What to do – Working in a group of 3 or 4, download from the internet emulators for the NES, the Atari 2600, the C64 and the Spectrum. Play a range of different games from different genres. As a group, compare your thoughts and experiences of the games that were available in the 80s and link these findings to the findings from Task 2.1. You could then write a presentation on your primary and secondary research findings.

BACK TO THE FUTURE: THE REVENGE OF THE CONSOLE – THE MEGA DRIVE AND THE PLAYSTATION

With the huge success of home computers such as the C64 and the Spectrum in the late 80s, it seemed that the future of gaming belonged to computers. But in the 1990s the videogame world turned again – back to consoles. The attack on the dominance of Commodore and Sinclair on the home video gaming market came from a variety of places – the Mega Drive, the Neo-Geo and, last but not least, the PlayStation. However, by no means was this a united front, and other bouts of platform wars lurked around the corner. While home computers became prominent and consoles fell out of the limelight in Europe; in Japan and the USA, the console flame kept burning. Nintendo's Famicom (Japanese name) / NES (western name) doing the lion's share of this work. The virtual collapse of Atari left the field open for players like Nintendo. The NES, launched in 1983, was a cartridge-oriented console; by the turn of the 80s, it was recognised that that particular dog had had its day, which is one reason why Nintendo had started to work with Sony on having a CD drive for loading games on what was mooted to become the Nintendo PlayStation. The CD platform for games offered greater storage capacity than cartridge which in turn meant better developed, longer games. Also, the storage capacity of CDs and quicker access times over loading games from tapes enabled this new wave of game consoles to establish themselves in the market at the same time that the C64 and Spectrum were starting to fade.

It was described earlier how the most common way of accessing games on the C64 (and the same was also true for the Spectrum) was by connecting the peripheral tape drive and loading games from tape. The new wave of consoles such as Sega's Mega Drive, SNK's Neo-Geo and Sony's PlayStation did away with this. The Sega Mega Drive wasn't this company's first foray into console manufacturing – in the 80s Sega had worked through a series of models – but the Mega Drive is lauded as the high point and knocked Nintendo of its perch in the American market. The success of consoles as the Mega Drive made cartridges look like Monopoly money and enabled new levels of sophistication to be reached in game design, ushering in a new era of game characters which have become stitched into the fabric of popular culture, such as *Sonic the Hedgehog*. Nintendo hit back and returned to the market with the Super NES, or SNES, and the two institutions locked horns in the handheld gaming market, with Sega launching the Game Gear to rival Nintendo's Game Boy.

The SNES, lauded for the range and quality of the games that supported the platform, was an instant hit on its home turf in Japan as the console's release was supported by the latest game in the *Mario Bros.* franchise, *Super Mario Bros 4*, which was bundled with the console when the SNES finally launched in the UK in 1992, nearly two years after its launch in Japan. The quality of the games produced by a wide range of developers for the console is a statement about the quality of the console and the numbers of consumers (developers only produce games for platforms where there is an audience to tap into). However, the SNES was born with the console equivalent of an Achilles' heel – games could only be loaded into the console in cartridge format. As Sega's Mega Drive had been first to market, arriving two years before the SNES, the CD genie was well and truly out of the bottle – there would be no going back.

SONY – THE NEW BOSS

It was this Achilles' heel that Sony exploited with the launch of the PlayStation in 1995. It was mentioned previously that originally the PlayStation was going to have been the Nintendo PlayStation, as at the turn of the 90s Nintendo and Sony were working together to produce a console which could play cartridge and CD games. Nintendo abruptly changed its mind leaving Sony to press on by itself with the PlayStation project. When the PlayStation arrived in 1995, it found itself competing with Sega's follow-up to the Mega Drive, the Saturn, which, like the PlayStation was a CD-only console. However, as the PS was cheaper, it is the PS that won that particular platform war and then the PS saw off Nintendo's N64 too. Sony was the new boss of the videogame industry.

TASK 2.4 – CLASH OF THE TITANS: THE SONY / NINTENDO FALL OUT

Objective – To consolidate your knowledge and understanding of the power struggles between institutions. This will develop your knowledge and understanding of the videogame industry from the institutional perspective.

What to do – Using www.google.com, run searches on 'Sony' and 'Nintendo'. Using a variety of sources, work out answers to the following questions:

- Why did Nintendo get twitchy about continuing its working relationship after the completion of prototypes for the Nintendo PlayStation?

- Why did Sony think cartridge-based consoles had had their shelf life by the early 1990s?

'FROM HERE TO ETERNITY'

The rise to dominance of Sony in the console market and the demise of Nintendo, following its colossal mistake not to keep pace with change in game delivery technology takes us to the close of the 1990s and to the cusp of the current decade and current century.

DAYS OF FUTURE PRESENT – 'NEXT GEN' BECOMES 'NOW GEN'

Hopefully, by now it will be clear that the road the videogame industry has taken from 'there' to 'here' is littered with casualties – most notably Atari and Commodore amongst others. Nintendo was added to that list as the 90s turned into the 00s. While players such as Atari and Commodore were long ago knocked out of the game, Nintendo was wounded but not quite down and out. We will survey the terrain of where the game is currently at.

Next gen / Now gen part 1 – PS2, XBox, Game Cube

In every generation of computers and game consoles, there comes a time when next generation becomes the present generation, a moment when the future slips into the present. In the 90s, when PlayStation established its dominance, and Nintendo belatedly rose to the threat of Sony with the N64 and Sega tried gamely with the Dream Cast, the coming next generation was the lure of the PS2 and in its wake Microsoft's entry into the console arena with the arrival of the XBox, with Nintendo settling for the budget market with the Game Cube. Writing in 2007, talking of these consoles as 'next gen' seems very old-fashioned, but in the run-up to the launches of these consoles, there was a lot of excitement in the industry and also amongst the audiences for games and consoles.

The PS2 launched in 2000, selling out all available consoles immediately. It has been consistently successful ever since its launch, as Sony has reduced the price and re-designed the PS2 to make it smaller – and then cut prices *again* (following the same pattern to success as it had achieved previously with the PS1). Taking an idea from what Nintendo had done with generations of its handheld Game Boy console series, the PS2 was made backwards compatible with PS1 titles, offering the potential buyer the incentive to trade up to play bigger and better games, but also offering you the facility to play your old games too – thereby spreading the potential target audience for the console through the demographic brackets (www.thocp.net/software/games/next_generation.htm). It was this kind of smart thinking that enabled Sony to become the boss of the videogame industry.

Until the launch of the XBox, Microsoft was best known for its Windows operating systems and software, such as Internet Explorer. Due to the burgeoning size of the videogame industry and the number of games that were being sold, and watching that number spiral upwards, Microsoft decided to act – enter the XBox. Similar to the PS2, the XBox offered the potential buyer not only a game console but also a DVD player. At the time of the launches of these game consoles, DVD players were relatively expensive, requiring an investment of at least £200 to secure you a good DVD player. In addition to that, the XBox offered internet connectivity, which the PS2 was always working towards, but never quite seemed to succeed, and a built-in hard drive that offered swifter processing and a more fluent gaming experience. Whilst arguably (and it's very arguable) the XBox ultimately had the better technical specification, the PS2 most certainly won the war – it has sold 117 million units to XBox's 24 million and compared to Game Cube's 21 million units. The figures for the XBox and the Game Cube are respectable – but the PS2, in terms of sales, is clearly in a different league (sales figures from http://en.wikipedia.org/wiki/Console_wars#World_wide_sales_figures_4, accessed on 18/6/07).

What these figures also show is how Nintendo has fallen – from bestriding the global stage in the 80s and early 90s with the Famicom / NES to bronze medal position in the 00s, at least until the launch of the Wii in the second half of the 'noughties'. It should also be noted that Nintendo's Game Cube was the last console to market for this generation – and this is undoubtedly a factor in why the Game Cube lags behind the big beast of Sony and the upstart Microsoft. Where the PS2 and the XBox both offered users the facility to play DVD discs on their consoles, the Game Cube did not – it seemed that Nintendo had not learned the lesson about moving with the times on the technology front. By this stage Nintendo had seemingly lost its way in the console wars and seemed to be spending more care and attention on its handheld gaming platforms – the Game Boy series and the new baby, the DS. The kind of games that were available for PS2 and XBox – such as *GTA 3* and *Halo* – simply weren't available for the Game Cube. This lack of very popular software meant Nintendo was always going to be struggling given the changes in the market for videogames, spreading through different demographic brackets.

At this point in time, Nintendo was no longer one of the major players in the console sector of the industry.

'Here we are now, entertain us': Next gen / Now gen part 2 – PS3, XBox 360, Wii, PSP

What is for certain is that analysing sales figures for the 7th generation consoles will not help us to learn very much at this point. It will be somewhere between late 2008 and 2010 when we know who the boss institution of the 7th generation is. However, with the aid of voices from within the videogame industry, in the final section of this chapter, we will explore some possible future directions for the videogame industry. To do this, we have some expert advice from veteran figures in different roles within the videogaming industry – Ian Dean, editor of *PSW* magazine in the UK, who is a seasoned veteran of videogame journalism, and John Foster, a designer on Sony's PlayStation Home.

The latest wave of next generation consoles has recently crashed ashore – first to market was the XBox 360, followed by Nintendo's radically new offering in the Wii. Uncharacteristically, Sony has been slower to market than it was with the PS2, as it has struggled to get its components right for launching the new version. Microsoft launched XBox 360 in 2005, with it hitting Europe in December of that year – just about making it to market for Christmas. As the PS3 didn't make it to market until 2007, the XBox 360 had the field to itself for the next year until Nintendo's Wii arrived in time for Christmas 2006. Its troubled development problems solved, the PS3 was finally launched in March of 2007. The patterns the three key consoles manufacturing institutions established with their 6th generation consoles have been replicated with their 7th generation – both Microsoft and Sony have added non-gaming high specification features to their consoles. Both consoles feature substantial hard drives which will allow you to use the PS3 and XBox 360 as an electronic storage device for photos, videos and music and both feature 'next gen' DVD players. Where they diverge is the type of DVD players they are incorporating – Sony incorporating Blu-ray DVD and Microsoft incorporating HD-DVD. It is possible that this latest (and final?) physical film delivery technology battle will have big implications as for which console and corporation emerges as the boss of the 7th generation. It is equally possible that the next gen DVD playback capabilities of these two big beasts will be the white elephant, especially if broadband internet connection speeds continue to increase, and legal and illegal downloading of films and TV programmes continue to grow – next gen DVD players may become obsolete. Also, equally possible is that the drivers of success for one or both of the two 'big beasts' of the console jungle, namely the XBox 360 and the PS3, will come from another source – such as the digital TV functionality to be added as purchasable peripherals for the two consoles, or perhaps, good old-fashioned word-of-mouth. As John Foster, Designer on PlayStation Home, of Sony Europe argues:

'Both Microsoft and Sony have also announced television services for their respective consoles, with the 360 delivering content over IP and the PS3 using a standard digital television signal, so that is a further area in which convergence is occurring. The PS3 also includes a relatively conventional web browser. If the aim of any console is to become the household "entertainment centre" I would expect future support for other entertainment technologies, the ability to synchronise an mp3 catalogue with a player for example.

With such developments, consoles are moving away from being "entertainment centres" and a better moniker might be "lifestyle centre", suggesting that future consoles may act in combination with what could be described as "life style accessories"; items such as mobile phones, music players, digital cameras and perhaps even GPS navigation units.' (Author interview.)

At the time of writing, word-of-mouth from students is that the XBox 360 is the way to go – but only time will tell. Nintendo, following its refusenik attitude towards incorporation of DVD playback facilities on the Game Cube has again elected to not have DVD players built into the Wii – although the Wii does offer the ability to connect to the internet. Is this a continuance of Nintendo's seeming perversity, ensuring all of its consoles come equipped with an Achilles' heel, or is it a smart move to not get sucked in to what could be a redundant battle? Perhaps Nintendo is better spending its time, energy and money on delivering a unique gaming experience – which my experience of talking to students shows that the Wii is succeeding in doing, reaching out to people who would not have previously thought of themselves as 'games players'.

Voices within the game industry offer a number of different arenas for the playing out of this battle between consoles, and between consoles and PCs for supremacy in gaming and in the larger and more lucrative field of home entertainment. Ian Dean, editor of the UK's *PSW* magazine, argues:

'Where will they go next? The battle is no longer one of hardware but software. Regular Firmware upgrades, offered free to gamers down the wire, unlock new functions with their hardware. These can be simple things, like adding backwards compatibility with old games (such as the PS3 offering the possibility of playing PS2 games and the Wii offering the ability to play GameCube games) or enabling wallpapers to be set and music playlists to be created.' (Author interview.)

These last named functions offer the consumer the possibility of customising and 'individualising' their console – in much the same way that mobile phones allow the user to customise and individualise through choosing your own ring tone by downloading mp3 tracks onto your phone and through enabling you to set wallpaper and screensavers from photos you've taken using your phone's camera function. Dean goes on to identify the reasons why consoles are increasingly being offered with a range of other functions beyond gaming:

'This is where we get to the battle for the living room. Both Microsoft and Sony have realised that the big bucks aren't made from hardcore gamers (these guys will buy the hardware and games regardless) but from the causal gamers, the mainstream. Nintendo's Wii has soared past XBox and PS3 in terms of hardware sales as it appeals to this very market — it's an exercise machine, a community hub and yes, a games machine too. But the big boys, Microsoft and Sony, hold the key to the future, with perhaps Sony sitting prettier. Years ago, back when the PS1 first launched against Sega's Saturn, the console's inventor rightly identified that Sega wasn't competition to where Sony planned to take gaming, but had picked out Microsoft as the main rival — around five years before XBox was released. This was because Sony wanted the mainstream. Sony has just revealed plans to release a PVR box for the PS3, effectively turning the PS3 into a set-top box — live digital TV can be watched and recorded, movies downloaded and you'll even be able to access you new PS3/TV on the bus by connecting wirelessly with your PSP over the internet. This is a massive step. The PS3 isn't a game console but a complex do-all entertainment system, enabling web surfing, gaming, music, TV and movie downloads, the works. The PSP itself will soon have a Skype function (web-videophone) email and GPS.'

Moving onto the issue of whether we are now entering the end-game for format wars, Dean states:

'Blu-ray has, by all accounts, won over against HD-DVD. The same strategy that helped sell DVDs into living rooms when the PS2 launched is working with PS3, do you buy a £1500 Sony Blu-ray player or the same player for £425 tucked into a PS3? From a games development angle, Blu-ray was always going to win, the larger storage capacity is becoming a necessity, with many developers now showing irritation at Microsoft's 'last gen' DVD tech. They simply can't fit the second wave of games onto one DVD. The deeper question of Blu-ray versus downloads is a complex one, on many scales. Sony wants developers to sell their games as downloads, via the Sony PSN Store, but presently the cost of a standard PS3 game can't be recouped from the small installed user base (an average game costs £30 million to develop, promote and produce). There has been a rise and eager take up in smaller, arcade games on both PSN and [XBox] Live — remakes of old coin-ops and HD versions of classics like *Street Fighter II* and *Mortal Kombat* — but these sell for £2.99 and not the £39.99 of a full price release. Gamers are eager to download but only up to a point. In the future downloading will take over, but this is 8 or 10 years away and undoubtedly lined up for PS4 and PS5. As I say, Sony wants people to download and is clearly using PS3 to set up the culture and hone the service, ready to reap the rewards in the future. Interestingly, the download concept works both ways — Sony has some games planned to encourage players to 'upload'. Next year sees the release of *Little Big Planet* a game construction kit rather than a game in its own right. Players will construct their own characters, levels, items, etc. and upload them to the shared server to play with other gamers. Sony's other project for next year is Home, an online persistent 3D world in which gamers can meet up, chat, play games, date, go to a virtual cinema and watch *Spider-Man 4*… the list is endless. The future of games is clearly edging towards a virtual space where there is no living room, except the one you make for yourself in your online home.' (Author interview.)

Within the fields of computing, software development and gaming, there is already a thriving 'home-brew' sub-culture where individuals shape and re-shape games and programmes for their own convenience, an infamous case was the 'hot coffee' incident in *GTA: San Andreas*, where by hacking into pieces of game code in the game but left out of the actual flow of the game's theoretically open-world, one could take a 'date' back to your *GTA* home for coffee and sexual seduction. Given that this 'home brew' culture is very much already alive and kicking, projects such as *Little Big Planet* most definitely have a substantial target audience. Also, in PS3's Home you have a very powerful rival to the social networking websites such as myspace.com and facebook.com.

REVELATIONS: 'I'VE SEEN THE FUTURE AND IT WORKS'

'Be Here Now' – technological convergence

Since the launch of consoles such as the PS1 and the others that have followed, it is clear that hardware manufacturers think it is imperative to achieve some convergence of different media technologies within the one 'box'. For example, with the PS1, you not only had a game console but also an audio CD player – which this writer found incredible at the time of launch of the PS1 in 1995. That process of convergence of different media technologies has gone into hyperdrive since then – the PS2 and XBox offered DVD playback facilities, and with the current generation, the PS3 offers convergence with DVDs, music, photos, videos and links to the PSP, which is not just a game console but essentially a highly developed, fairly portable total media player. Similarly, the XBox 360 is offering a similar range of features. How far can this process go? When the 8th generation of consoles starts to appear, probably somewhere around 2010–12 judging by the gap between previous generations, what extra possible features will they sport? Will the next gen actually be a console as we currently know it or will it be a total home entertainment and business management package – essentially an amalgam of game console combined with top-end specification PC? What kinds of different sub-markets might open up with the growing trend to convergence?

In response to the question about whether the future of gaming lies with consoles or PCs, John Foster from Sony wasn't so sure that this distinction was as straightforward as you might think, arguing:

'I am not sure that a distinction [between consoles and PCs] can be simply made. Whether a given hardware platform fits into one of the categories above or another could easily be debated, as each category is really just a term invented to apply to a device that provides a certain expected range of applications and abilities, and the exact range of abilities expected of each category is still easily the subject of debate. At what point does a fully featured game console become an entertainment system or a home PC?' (Author interview.)

In response to the same question, Ian Dean from *PSW* magazine argues:

'It's clearly with consoles. The PS3 is more powerful than any current PC and if you want the features of a PC you can upload the Linux operating system. Both PS3 and XBox 360 can connect to your PC wirelessly, so if you want to watch that movie stored on your PC, you can, but now on your HD TV in your living room. As for cost, the 360 is likely to be £199 in the near future with PS3 likely hitting £299. As technology becomes cheaper to develop (i.e. the custom tools needed to construct the chips), costs are lowered. As the consoles functions widen, those prices look very cheap – a stand-alone Blu-ray player is still costing you over £1000.' (Author interview.)

Convergence of different media technologies is supposed to be the Holy Grail – but is it? The path that Nintendo is carving out with the Wii certainly suggests that not all corporations are looking for total convergence. Perhaps there will be some recognition that there are limits to what a game console can do or should try to do. Herein lays a possible untapped market. For example, in just about every house in Britain you will find at least one stereo. The chances are that the stereo system will do more than one thing – it will probably feature a combination of CD player and tuner at the very least. Depending on the age and sophistication of the unit, it may also incorporate a tape deck and / or a turntable. However, these types of combination 'midi' system do not represent the whole of the market; there is also a big market for hi-fi separates – where in one box you have a tuner, in another you have an amp and so on. Building up a stereo system this way offers the user a fair degree of control about what to have and how and when to upgrade components, in the same way that PCs offer some degree of control about what to update (sound card, graphics cards, external hard drives). So the technological direction of the industry is not clear cut and could, and to some extent at least, probably will go in a number of different directions as different corporations find themselves selling to different segments of consumers and audiences.

The Last Battle: The end of platform wars?

Of course, what is outlined above implies we will continue to consume media products in roughly the same ways as we do now. Whether you want access to a videogame, a CD or DVD, the easiest way to get access to that content is to go to a shop, or visit an online shop, and make a purchase. You then access the content by placing the media into the relevant hardware device and off you go. Throughout this chapter frequent reference has been made to platform wars. It is conceivable that in the great battle currently underway between PS3, XBox 360 and the Wii, we are witnessing the last of the great platform wars that have been raging in the industry since the late 1970s. Perhaps the future lies in pure internet downloading of games – as is now possible on the networks attached to all three of the 7th generation consoles. Indeed, it is currently Sony's aim to move its internet provision towards more focused support and more availability of PS3 content than always seeking to expand access to PS1 and PS2 games by download. As broadband connection speeds increase, will we want to have to keep buying physical media which takes up storage space in homes or will we shift to online storage of games and movies and TV programmes, where we don't physically own anything? We simply rent content when we want it – a futuristic equivalent of going to a video rental store and renting a DVD and a videogame for a couple of days.

rEalitY: 'Gimme Some Truth' or Theatre of Dreams?

The final area for consideration is what changes await with the development of videogames themselves. In 1999, the David Cronenberg film eXistenZ was released – this film was set within a virtual reality called 'eXistenZ'. By the end of the film the characters had hopped through so many layers of games and what purported to be reality, that they and the spectator didn't know if and when they had reached the 'real world' – possibly they were locked in a game somewhere unable to get out. They were locked in because so many aspects of the games were so real that the characters couldn't differentiate between real world and game world, the fear that anti-games commentators have about today's games (see Chapter 4 for further details). With the development of higher technical specifications for game consoles and ever better facilities for game development, might we get to a stage where the world of eXistenZ comes about? Would it be personally and socially desirable that gamers live their lives by proxy so much that they might lose sight of who they are and what they are? Surely people will always know they're playing a game…won't they?

Accounting for why there is movement to a sense of realism in games, where the rules of game worlds bear some relation to the rules of the real world, Ian Dean argues:

'Games are getting real because gamers are getting older. Those 8-year-olds that played on their Atari 2600s are now in their mid 30s, and still playing games. There were and have always been "mature" games though, and even offensive games. In the old Atari 2600 game Custer's Revenge (also called Westward Ho!) you had to get across the screen and romp with a bound Native American woman tied to a post – your on-screen hero Custer had a visible erection.

Obviously this was a crude and offensive game, the difference now is that games cost more than your average Hollywood movie (and make more revenue) and so aren't made by frustrated teenagers but adults, adults with concepts and influences that draw on pop culture and politics – *GTA IV's* central character is an Eastern European illegal immigrant, Vivendi's forthcoming *Prototype* comments on the idea of identity in modern America. Obviously you shoot people and collect stuff, but amidst the action are deeper messages that engage with the player. The likes of Clive Barker, Peter Jackson and Steven Spielberg are all making games on PS3 and XBox 360 because they can create worlds and messages. It's a matter of perspective, *Transformers the Movie* is childish, *The Departed* is a mature movie with a message, the games equivalent would be *Hideo Kojima's Metal Gear Solid* series or the *GTA* titles.

Realism in games isn't so much about striving for photorealism but trying to achieve a feeling of realism. *GTA 3*, *Half-Life 2* and *BioShock* aren't 'real' but within their own worlds realism is alluded to – day turns to night, jobs accepted and relationships formed. I'd say it's more about creating worlds that set their own rules and stick to them than creating our world in exact detail. In fact, those games that do attempt to recreate real locations, such as Sony's *The Getaway*, fail because reality is no place for fun game design – real roads are designed to slow you down at corners, game roads are designed to maintain speed.

Where the line could blur is with peripherals such as the Wii remote, where gamers act out the action of the on-screen hero – you're no longer a passive observer looking at the TV but directly interacting with the TV. All fine if the games, current as they are, involve cooking, bowling and tennis, but Rockstar's *Manhunt 2* put you in the shoes of a killer, a violent serial killer to be exact and you then "acted out" the motions of stabbing, strangulation and hacking – it was dubbed a murder simulator and then banned by the BBFC [later overturned].' (Author interview.)

On the note of what actually constitutes realism in games, John Foster argues:

'Firstly, I believe a distinction can be made between "realism" in terms of serving the senses and "realism" in terms of what a player actually believes they are experiencing. For example, a player can observe a game scene showing a fish swimming through water and they may think "that looks so realistic, it looks just like a real fish swimming in real water", but at no time might they actually believe they are seeing anything other than computer generated imagery. Alternatively, a player may hear a relatively low-fi audio feed of a radio broadcast and for whatever reason believe that what they are hearing is a real radio broadcast being piped into a game from an external source.

There is certainly a push toward providing high fidelity graphics in games. I don't believe this pursuit is a new trend, however. I simply think that technology has now reached a point where scenes of a semi-realistic nature can be presented. So it used to be that graphics got "nicer" with each new hardware generation; now we can begin to replace the word "nicer" with the word "realistic".

As far as the other approach to realism in games, there are very few games that attempt to blur the line between what is actually real and what has been created by the game developers. The example titles below attempt to blend the two to some degree by basing their murder mystery games on a mixture of created evidence and real-world websites. By this method the developers play at suggesting that the game events are in some way real, though whether any players fully absorb this illusion is probably more dependant on their own state of mind:

http://www.adventurecompanygames.com/tac/missing/index.html

http://www.adventurecompanygames.com/tac/evidence/index.html

It is safe to say that this kind of game is pretty rare among its peers, and so it might be said that there is in fact no actual push for greater reality in games. Rather there is a push for more impressive theatre.' (Author interview.)

The Never-Ending Story – game genres and future developments

The history of every medium is, in part, a history of the rise and fall of genres – the rise and fall of genres is a marker for institutional developments, industrial upheavals and societal changes. A look at the history of the western genre in American film, and its peaks and troughs of financial and critical success, is one avenue for investigation. The developments of the music programme and reality genres in British TV are also symptomatic of their industrial climate and audience needs and desires. The same is also true for the videogame industry, the institutions that comprise and the audiences / consumers of the texts that the industry produces. In response to a question about the impact of technological innovation on gaming hardware and software, our two industry experts had the following points to offer. Ian Dean sees the shadow of the *GTA* series looming large, arguing that:

'The open-world genre typified by *GTA* is the genre of this and the last console generation. Since *GTA 3* most publishers were happy to release makeshift gangster games, set in free-roaming cities; you choose your story, missions and objectives in a 'real' world. On PS3 and XBox 360 developers are opening up the concept and applying it to more genres, so you have *Oblivion*, a free roaming RPG, or *Prototype*, a free roaming super hero game, or *Alan Wake*, a free roaming horror adventure. Freedom is the new genre if any there were, gamers want realistic behaving worlds and choice to explore and develop their skills at their pace. The next step is to apply *GTA*'s methods to online gaming, co-op adventures in which you team up across the globe. People will always want racing, shooting and platform games; RPG, adventure and puzzle genres, but more than likely wrapped in a free-foam environment where they can dip in and out of each at their will.' (Author interview.)

Offering an alternative to this is John Foster, seeing a bright future for party games:

'Games such as Wii *Sports* and *SingStar* have to some extend created renewed interest in party games. A party game can be defined in many ways, but perhaps two of the most important factors are as follows.

1. A single session of a party game is very short lived, making it easy to pick up for just a few minutes if required. This also makes it suitable for group play, where time spent purely as a spectator ("waiting your turn") is relatively minimal.

2. A party game requires very little practice for meaningful participation, enabling it to form the basis of impromptu group activity among a variety of participants.

A comparison with the film world shows generally that all genres peak and trough in popularity, but that the reason behind any given variance is often quite insubstantial. One good game in any given genre can boost the popularity of that genre, as well of the subsequent number of games published in an effort to cash in on the same success.' (Author interview.)

Perhaps it is the very 'quickness' and lack of immersion that have led to the growth of the party game genre – running totally counter to the nightmare visions of gaming expressed in films such as *eXistenZ*. Writing in the run-up to Christmas 2007, what is beyond doubt is the current popularity of party games – the shelves of game departments are bulging with *SingStar* games, *Buzz* games and *Guitar Hero* games. Wherever this never-ending story takes us, it seems that for the videogame industry the future is one in which this industry will now always be with us – this is not a fad, a phase, a moment of temporary insanity – gaming is here to stay. Game on.

TASK 2.5 – 2020 VISION

Objective – To draw together your understanding of the history of the videogames industry and the interactions between audiences and institutions.

What to do – Imagine it is 2020 and you are writing a history of the videogames industry from 7th generation consoles onwards to 2020. What developments have unfolded? What institutions are dominant and why? Which institutions have fallen by the wayside and why? How are playing games? Do games consoles still exist?

GAME OVER

At this end of the chapter you should have a good idea of the milestones in the development of the videogame history to date. You should be very familiar with names such as Atari, Commodore, Spectrum, Nintendo, Sony and Microsoft. With completion of the tasks, you should also have a secure knowledge and understanding of how the issues raised in this chapter have affected the fortunes of the different institutions involved and how the game playing public has responded, and hopefully you had some fun along the way with playing 80s games through emulators!

3. THE SOCIAL EFFECTS OF VIDEOGAMES

Playing the first chapter of *The Godfather* on PSP, the player quickly works out the narrative and her /.his place within it. In order to progress through the ranks of the organised crime 'family', your avatar must coerce, corrupt, bully and extort a range of shopkeepers and small business owners. This is to gain 'respect'. Sometimes violence is required, sometimes not, and one of the first skills the player needs to develop is working this out. It is not a good idea to use violence when this is unnecessary – senior members of the family will not be impressed by this. For the player who is familiar with *The Godfather* films, this is a familiar narrative and thus the use of violence is taken for granted – this is the world the text occupies. Both the films and the videogame feature graphic violence. The violence is a means to an end and thus legitimised to some extent. But is the player likely to act more violently in the 'real world' as a result of playing the game? And is this more likely for the videogame player than for the film viewer, due to the more interactive relationship with the text offered by the PSP?

We will try to maintain balance in this chapter. Ultimately, as a student of videogames you will take an informed, critical perspective on their social effects. But it must be said from the outset that there is a long-standing division between those concerned with 'effects' who tend to base their worries on the outcomes of psychological research experiments which use highly specific and artificial research methods and Media Studies academics who see the relationship between texts and their 'readers' as much more complex. Even more troubling is the fact that a great deal of 'research' published specifically about the dangers of videogames is not based on any 'scientific' evidence at all. And because children are usually the focus of the discourse of concern over media effects, this is a highly emotive topic which means it gets a disproportionate amount of media attention itself, leading to a wider public debate based on scarce real evidence. Craig and Petley (1998) argue that in many cases, the conclusions of research in this area are decided before the 'experiments' are actually conducted. Game enthusiasts are so familiar with the ways in which they are 'demonised' that they enjoy parodying the media hype; *Playstation Plus* magazine even ran a spoof story on one April Fool's Day about a fictional new violent game just to court negative attention from the press (it worked).

The title of this chapter refers to the social effects of games. It is useful firstly to distinguish between psychological and sociological approaches to effects and, secondly, to bring them together for our purposes. Broadly speaking psychological theories relate to what is going on in the mind of the individual human being when immersed in a game, whilst sociological theories look at the broader impact of games on groups of people or society in general. In practice the two come together because a psychological effect on a human being that leads to a change in behaviour will lead to consequences for others, and if this effect is shared by a number of people, then the wider society may change.

John Stuart Mill (1806–73) was a political philosopher who we wouldn't usually associate with videogames but we can apply his ideas to make this point more clearly. In trying to work out how to judge human behaviours (which ones should be allowed in a society based on liberty and freedom), Mill distinguished between self-regarding and other-regarding behaviours or practices. Mill said that human beings in a free society should be allowed to do anything they like as long as it does not affect others in a negative way. But judging this is not as easy as it might seem. Consider the debate over recent legislation to ban smoking in public places. This new law is based on the idea that smoking is other-regarding, as research has proven that passive smoking can contribute to cancer and heart disease. But many smokers argue that they are only harming themselves. Driving whilst under the influence of alcohol, on the other hand, is clearly other-regarding. If you stretch Mills' theory you can come up with an example like this:

> There is nothing wrong with a drunken prostitute riding a motorbike without a helmet in the privacy of his or her home.

If you have a discussion with friends in response to this statement, you will find that people will disagree over whether the person in this example is only putting her / himself in danger, and whether it is likely that these actions, whilst essentially self-regarding, might lead to or be connected to other-regarding actions. Or whether being drunk or selling oneself or putting oneself in danger might have effects on others that are indirect. For example, if the prostitute is killed, will others be affected – does this person have children? What this (admittedly extreme example) illustrates is that it is never very easy to work out whether individual behaviour is limited to effects on that individual. Where does the individual end and society begin? For this reason, we can say that psychological approaches to gaming will always be connected to sociological ideas.

MORAL PANICS

In September 2006 110 teachers, psychologists, children's authors and other experts wrote a collective letter to the *Daily Telegraph* (12 September 2006) newspaper expressing their concerns about the rise in childhood mental illness. In the letter this group distinguished between 'real' food and 'junk' food and also between 'real' play as opposed to sedentary, screen-based entertainment. According to the authors of this letter, videogames are part of the problem, and the problem is a fairly serious one – that *'the mental health of an unacceptable number of children is being unnecessarily compromised'*.

ACTIVITY 3.1

Using the internet and a range of other media over one week, collect examples of people expressing concern about videogames. These might be related to health, schoolwork, violence, addiction to games, effects on eyesight or other negative outcomes of playing videogames. When you have gathered a range of material, identity which of the examples are based on evidence or research and which are based on assumptions or attitudes.

In 1972 Stanley Cohen published his 'moral panic' theory, suggesting that one way in which societies reproduce and maintain a set of social norms is to exaggerate the 'dangers' at a relatively early stage of developing types of behaviour that might threaten the society's 'normal' codes of behaviour. Whilst these can be associated with a wide range of cultural practices, it is often the behaviour of youth that is 'panicked' over, and in many cases this is connected to extreme reactions to popular culture, whether this be music, films, television or more recently videogames. Part of Cohen's theory relates to his idea of the 'deviancy amplification spiral' which leads to the public's perception of the potentially dangerous behaviour being blown out of proportion by a combination of the media, politicians and authority figures. An example of what Cohen might see as a 'moral panic' might be the work of Dave Lt. Col. Grossman (of the 'Killology Research Group') and Gloria Degaetano whose book *Stop Teaching Our Kids to Kill* claims that the makers of 'shoot em up' videogames are directly responsible for youth gun crime in America, as they have effectively trained the players to shoot people in real life. However, you are free to decide whether you think these authors have a point – you might see their thesis as a genuine, evidence-based attempt to save lives rather than a 'moral panic'.

McDougall and Duncan (2008) conducted some research with primary school students in the West Midlands, and began by asking them which games they were currently playing:

'The most common games listed as current favourites were *Mortal Kombat* (18), *Harry Potter* (3+), *Resident Evil 4* (16), *LA Rush* (12), *X-Men* (12), *Grand Theft Auto: San Andreas* (18), *Simpsons* (7+) and *Cricket 2005* (3+). Legally, these children should only have been playing 2 of these 8 games, and whilst (other) data about access to consoles suggests that these games were owned by older siblings or friends, this is still evidence that the classification system is ineffective in gatekeeping access to the kinds of games that are central to the "discourse of concern".' (McDougall and Duncan, 2007: 3)

Generally speaking, there seems to be widespread agreement that videogames have an effect of some sort. Opinion in this area ranges from those who wish to ban games because they think there is a direct link between violent games and violent behaviour to those who think playing games too often stops children from doing exercise and socialising. On the other hand, there is a developing school of thought suggesting gaming might actually be making people literate in new ways and cognitively 'sharper'. In this section we will review this range of debates but try to avoid taking 'media effects' for granted. Indeed we will even dare to ask – might videogames have no tangible or 'knowable' affect whatsoever?

LOST REALITY?

Second Life: *A product derived of substance?*

Here we can go beyond questions about the effects of games on individual players or even social groups and go into deeper debates about the nature of human thought. Videogames are sometimes labelled 'postmodern'. This is because they are seen to subvert our traditional ideas about the distinction between reality and simulation or image. Recent game world experiences such as *Second Life* take this even further, offering the participant the opportunity to purchase virtual land with real money. What is the effect of this on our human identity and consciousness? The philosopher Slavoj Žižek (often associated with postmodernism) makes the following observation in response to this:

'Virtual reality simply generalises the procedure of offering a product derived of its substance, of the hard resistant kernel of the Real – just as decaffeinated coffee smells and tastes like real coffee without being real coffee, Virtual reality is experienced as reality without being so. What happens at the end of this process of virtualization, however, is, that we begin to experience 'real reality' itself as a virtual entity.' (Žižek, 2002, in Easthope and McGowan, 2005: 231)

ACTIVITY 3.2

Immerse yourself (we will come to a discussion on the nature of immersion later) in a videogame of your choice. Play it for hours. Then, at a planned time, stop abruptly and immediately write, record or dictate a one minute monologue reflection on the 'reality' you have just been immersed in. Does your monologue seem to support Žižek's view that what you have been doing is 'decaffeinated'?

JUNK CULTURE?

When videogames are discussed in terms of their negative effects, particularly on children, an analogy with food is often used – the idea of children being fed a 'diet of junk media'. But the difference is that we can easily calculate the effects of a person's food diet on their health by assessing their weight, body shape, heart rate, blood pressure and cholesterol but the outcomes of gaming are less straightforward to measure. This is because most speculation is about attitudes and feelings rather than behaviours – the notion that playing violent games makes us 'desensitised' to real violence is hard to prove, apart from in the very rare instances where people commit violent crime and state a game as the influential factor. But even then, how do we work out whether the person's mental state was healthy in the first place, before the game 'corrupted' them?

To return to the dietary theme, there is also a concern about the relationship between sedentary consumption of electronic media (and it is usually TV and games that are used as examples) and obesity, as expressed here by sports science researchers:

> 'It is commonly accepted that media-based sedentary behaviours such as TV viewing and video game use compete for time that would otherwise be spent in physical activity, which might lead to obesity.' (Mota et al., 2006: 8)

> While there is no doubt that video game play … is a sedentary activity, the stark fact is that many young people spend as much time playing games as they do their homework.' (Crowe and Bradford, 2007: 15)

It is obvious that any sedentary activity is likely to have a detrimental impact on calorie expenditure if undertaken in excess (whilst exercise is rarely or never taken), and that any activity (including sport, actually) will have a negative impact on homework if disproportionate time is taken up by the activity and little time is left for study. Ironically, then, swimming could be a contributory factor in academic under-achievement and studying could have a harmful impact on physical health. But the concern about videogames is based on the notion that players become so engrossed / immersed / 'addicted' to playing games that they are likely to spend more time on this activity than any other, if parents do not intervene. Is this the case in reality?

ACTIVITY 3.3

In a group of three or four, each conduct some micro-research with a different group of ten regular videogame players who are studying for exams. Ask them to keep a journal of how they spend their time outside of school during a normal school week (time spent studying, going out, playing videogames, eating, sleeping, taking part in sport or other activities, watching TV, using the internet, reading – whichever categories you think work best for this). Bring the data back to the group, collate it and write up the conclusions – make sure you summarise the information in terms of the averages and also the extremes – if one person plays for eight hours a day but this is far more than any other person in the sample, state this as it will skew the average. Overall, would the data you have gathered seem to support the views expressed in the quotes above from Mota et al, Crowe and Bradford?

Some recent research has even offered a challenge to the assumption that games are inevitably 'unhealthy'. Researchers in the West Midlands conducted an experiment in a primary school, attaching heart rate monitors to children whilst they played Eye Toy games during their lunch break. This data was compared to that taken from children engaging in a PE lesson and those playing outside during the break:

> 'In regard to heart rate monitoring, active video game play resulted in favourable physical activity profile that is comparable or better than heart rate values recorded for regular daily physical activity or regular school lunch time physical activity. In this instance, the use of active video game play appears promising as an alternative method to enhance children's physical activity. Considering that physical activity during active game play is greater than general lunch time activity and physical activity following playground based interventions, it may be prudent for the scientific / health / educational communities to consider the potential uses of active video gaming in promoting physical activity or attracting children who are not physically active to activity in a different way.' (McDougall and Duncan, 2007: 5)

COULD READING BE BAD FOR YOU?

Here is a simple question that hardly ever gets asked – is there a negative physical outcome of reading novels? Don't we sit in pretty much the same position when we read a book as we do when we play a videogame? And of course the new range of kinaesthetic games are clearly more physical than book reading. The reason that novels are never condemned for their contribution to either obese or antisocial youth is simple – novels are considered culturally more 'valuable' and (rightly or wrongly) the reader is assumed to be active – using the imagination, whereas the viewer of television or the gamer is assumed to be passive (being 'dumbed' down').

Kendall (2008) describes dominant ideas about the value of cultural choices, which serve to 'articulate a "common sense" about different types of texts, their value (in capital terms) and the worth of engaging with them.' (2008: 5)

Steven Johnson (2005) turns this around cleverly in his book *Everything Bad is Good for You* by imagining what our ideas of cultural value might look like if videogames had come before novels:

> 'Reading books chronically understimulates the senses. Unlike the longstanding tradition of game playing – which engages the child in a vivid, three-dimensional world filled with moving images and musical soundscapes, navigated and controlled with complex muscular movements – books are simply a barren string of words on the page. Only a small portion of the brain devoted to processing written language is activated during reading, while games engage the full range of the sensory and motor cortices.' (Johnson, 2005: 19)

Of course, as Johnson knows, it's not that simple and we have to distinguish between games and between books – some are more stimulating than others, but even then it depends on the cultural experience and preferences of the player / reader in each case. The problem is that people do tend to lump games together due to the relative infancy of the medium (including us – would you buy a book called *Studying Books?*).

GAMING AND LITERACY

> 'One of the most striking and ominous features of our present cultural situation is the division between the technical languages of the experts and the extraordinarily low level of the organs of mass communication.' (Hoggart, 1961: 11)

Writing in the early 1960s, Richard Hoggart's seminal book *The Uses of Literacy* attempted to describe the impact of literacy on working class people and in so doing he spelled out his views on the dangers of mass produced popular culture in eroding the value of this new found access to the written word. Hoggart's position is still highly influential today, with many critics of television, tabloid newspapers, new technologies and videogames taking the same stance. The view seems to be that the 'masses' are in danger of throwing away the benefits of their education by consuming a diet of debased culture.

So it is that within a broader discussion of possible 'effects' of videogames, we come to turn our attention to the challenge this media form poses for theories of literacy.

ACTIVITY 3.4

In a group of six, each start a mini-essay by completing this sentence: 'A literate person is able to…'. Now pass your essay clockwise to the person next to you. After their first sentence, complete this one: 'Therefore it follows that an illiterate person…'. Continue this process with the next four sentences, passing the essay clockwise in between each one:

'However, literacy these days includes not only reading and writing written text but also…'.

'These new media forms change literacy by…'.

'But critics of new media and technology argue that…'.

'"In conclusion, …"'

After the six sentence essay is complete, you should have your original essay back (the first sentence should be yours). What you should now have is a collective first attempt to set out the debate on new literacies.

Kathleen Tyner (1998) draws our attention to what she calls the 'disconnect' between the kinds of literacy favoured by the school system and the kinds of literacy people are engaged in when they access new media forms and new technologies. In particular, the 'adult culture' often dismisses forms of new media literacy such as texting, social networking on the internet and videogame playing as being 'illegitimate' forms of textual practice, as Kendall's quote above shows us. For Tyner, the purposes of literacy are changing as well, but ideas about what is and what isn't literacy are never neutral:

> 'Once a literary shift is set in motion, it gathers its own momentum. Questions about whether the changes in literacy practices are for the better or for the worse depend on the loyalties and vantage point of the questioner. Who has a voice, what content is available, who receives it, how it is interpreted, and how information is used are questions that ebb and flow throughout the history of literacy.' (Tyner, 1998: 17)

James Paul Gee, who we will pay more attention to later in this chapter when we explore the classroom response to videogames, is very clear about the change in literacy practice put in motion by this medium:

> 'When people learn to play video games, they are learning a new literacy. Of course, this is not the way "literacy" is normally used. Traditionally, people think of literacy as the ability to read and write. Why, then, should we think of literacy more broadly, in regard to video games or anything else for that matter?' (Gee, 2003: 14)

Gee goes on to answer his own question by suggesting that visual literacy is equally important today to the need to decode the printed word, and that words and images these days are usually connected – understanding this is called *mutimodal* literacy.

Lankshear and Knobel (2006) call this new kind of literacy 'remix'. They claim that literacy practices are far more important than texts or documents – in other words, people who have 'grown up digital' (from Tapscott, 1998) are able to easily navigate, decode and reshape a range of multimodal information in a non-linear way. But this is a fluid active practice, meaning there isn't a stable, fixed text for us to assess at any one time. To understand this we have to reconfigure how we think of literacy to get our heads around the idea that reading is increasingly to do with working within complex systems of information:

> 'We know beyond a shadow of doubt that human beings are hardwired to manage systems. We see evidence of them doing so whenever we read accounts of young people's gaming practices.' (Lankshear and Knobel, 2006: 254)

So if we take these claims seriously (and you would need to follow up the references here to get a more secure, informed view, of course), we might say that one social effect of videogames is the development of a range of more complex, systematic literacies than were at work when Hoggart was writing. So it wouldn't make much sense to say either that videogame players are more or less literate as a result of their immersion in, or even addiction to, virtual worlds. Instead we would have to conclude that they are just *differently* literate.

'EVERY CHILD MATTERS'

The UK's Children's Act of 2004 came about largely as a result of the death of Victoria Climbie, a child who died as a result of a lack of communication between education, health and social work professionals. A new 'inter-agency' approach was subsequently established by the Government policy document 'Every Child Matters'. One of the key criteria for safeguarding children in both the act and the policy document is 'Being Healthy'. British readers will be aware of the highly publicised campaign led by the celebrity chef Jamie Oliver for healthier school meals which partly led to the development of a 'Healthy Schools Initiative' linked to 'Every Child Matters'. But alongside this, there is a connection between this desire to make children physically healthier with a desire to make children emotionally and mentally healthy. Ofcom, the UK regulatory body for the communications industry, has in response imposed a ban on the advertising of junk food to children and created a media literacy strategy which aims to help children to make 'safer' media consumption choices. Inevitably videogames are a key focus in this agenda. Whilst Ofcom does not regulate the games industry and thus their interest is more on broadcasting and the internet, it does include several statements in its 'Media Literacy Bulletins' (available at www.ofcom.org.uk) about how a media literate person might respond to a videogame, within this broader definition of media literacy. One such statement defining Media Literacy is:

> '...the ability to access, understand and create communications in a variety of contexts.'

The Institute of Education's Centre for the Study of Children, Youth and Media was consulted on Ofcom's agenda and offered the following response:

'(Media literacy) goes well beyond the ability to protect oneself from potentially harmful or dangerous material. It needs to be seen in its widest sense as a cultural phenomenon – associated with taste, aesthetic discrimination, the appreciation of media texts, and the artistic and creative dimensions of media forms and technologies. Many media forms such as video games are more accurately characterised as forms of imaginative narrative. The implication for media literacy is that forms of critical engagement need to be fostered; but so do pleasure, appreciation and creative production.' (www.ofcom.org.uk/consult/condocs – accessed 7 April 2008)

The researchers at the Institute were arguing here that the Ofcom definition of the 'consumer' was too limited, and didn't bear witness to the complexity of media audiences' interactions with games in particular. This brings us to the 'effects debate' which we must engage with if we are to view the social impacts of games through a sufficiently critical lens.

MEDIA AUDIENCE THEORIES

The effects approach is just one of a wide range of paradigms that media researchers work within and between. Whilst there is some debate now amongst media academics, in particular Buckingham (2000) and Gauntlett (2007), it is useful here to lay out some key models before moving on to review effects in more detail. Ferguson (2003) offers a helpful summary, distinguishing between audience theory (thinking about how audiences are constructed) and audience research (trying to provide evidence for how audiences respond to media). So research is best understood as trying to provide supporting evidence for a theory. Some examples of audience theories are as follows.

One extreme variant of effects theory is the **hyperdermic syringe** model which viewed audiences as passive recipients of 'injected' messages – whilst this might seem outdated now, we will look later at the work of Grossman on videogames and you might conclude that his view fits with this idea. Another effects idea is **cultivation theory** – audiences develop views of the world over time as an exposure to media, views which may be 'distorted'. Another is **desensitisation** – the more mediated violence we are exposed to, the less shocked we are by it in real life. And another is **copycat theory** – this idea of people acting out what they see 'modelled' in the media is the part of effects theory that gets the most coverage (famous cases include the Jamie Bulger murder in Liverpool and the Columbine killings in the US). More complex audience theories include **uses and gratifications** (although again this is a little outdated now) which turns our attention more to what the audience 'do' with the media (how they use it for their needs); **reception theory** (audiences make different, plural (polysemic) meanings from the starting points of texts, and these meanings will depend on their socio-cultural experiences and situations); **ethnography** (looking at how audience members are situated before and by texts); and **postmodern theory** (which rejects the traditional distinction between reality and media reality / representation). The challenging view of Gauntlett (2007) is that new media erodes the boundary between producer and audience to the extent that it makes little sense to talk about media audiences in this way anymore – he calls this rethink 'Media Studies 2.0'.

MEDIA EFFECTS

We can't begin to explore the debates around the possible 'effects' of videogames on players without first being sure we understand the media effects debate in a broader sense. This is not an area where everyone agrees by any means, and there tends to be discord between three voices – those who articulate their concerns about the effects of the media without any actual evidence; those who have conducted research into media effects (whether the outcomes are positive or negative); and those who are the subject of the debate, usually children or teenagers consuming new forms of media which the 'adult culture' are worrying about (whether it's gangsta rap, social networking on the internet, slasher movies or videogames).

A crucial contextual fact we must take into account here is this – most gamers are not teenage boys. Before we even start analysing the claims made about harmful effects on the audience, we need to question the assumptions made about 'who' that audience actually are, never mind how they think. Newman (2003: 50) found that the audience for games are generally 'not defined through empirical research but rather "read" or "implied" from the text of the videogame'. Whilst there is certainly a rather old-fashioned (if not downright offensive) demarcation of gender targeting around games, there is a growing female community of gamers, and the Interactive Digital Software Association recently reported that the average game player is 28 years of age. Even more complex is the nature of 'consumption' – whereas the audience for a film can be straightforwardly gauged from a combination of box office, DVD sales and rentals, downloads and scheduled TV ratings, it is much harder to work out who is playing games and how. One reason for this is that games are often examples of media convergence, so it is difficult to see where the consumption of the game begins and ends in relation to other media texts that the game relies on or links to. Also, there are many more players than purchasers of games and the variety of playing approaches are extraordinary in comparison to television, for example. Here, Newman wrestles with just one aspect – the question of a player moving through a level:

'Typically, levels do not take a specific period of time to complete, and thus the total duration of the level may be as dependent on the player's ability as on the content of the game per se. Remember also that it may take the player several attempts to complete the level. Even what we mean by complete has a bearing on the amount of time taken.' (2004: 58)

To add yet more complexity (frustrating but infinitely more productive than opting for misguided simplicity), game theorists are writing about the fundamental importance of *immersion* in the gaming experience, but there is disagreement over the extent to which this immersion in the game whilst playing is passive or active (assuming the former experience carries more potential for 'harm'):

'Intense computer game play is often described in terms of a loss of a sense of time, of place, or self – of immersion. However the immersion of the computer game player is less the submersion in virtual reality as the quality of intense concentration produced by having to attend to a combination of activities – mastering control systems, figuring out the gameplay, puzzle solving, enemy slaying and strategic planning. The contradiction between immersion as passive / active reveals a complex set of desires and anxieties around technology in general, and computer games in particular. Immersion is clearly offered as a fundamental aspect of gameplay experience and pleasure, yet it also figures as potentially the most problematic element within that experience. The same tensions have existed in relation to earlier cultural and media forms, including but not limited to literature, cinema and television. Each offers the promise of immersion, yet each is provocative of particular kinds of anxiety around readers / viewers / users / players who are too immersed.' (Dovey and Kennedy, 2006: 9)

GROWING UP ELECTRONIC

Returning to the theme of the 'digital generation', a range of writers (including Livingstone, Tapscott and Buckingham) have offered more positive perspectives than the views expressed in the letter to the *Telegraph* we considered earlier. David Buckingham's *After the Death of Childhood* dismantles a range of the 'deficit model' claims made about contemporary childhood in relation to electronic media. Buckingham argues that childhood itself is a social construction rather than a fixed, stable entity and as such it is difficult for adults to discuss it without recourse to nostalgia or simplistic 'black and white' thinking:

'Contemporary views of children's relationships with the media are two contrasting forms of sentimentality. On the one hand, there is an old, familiar sentimentality – a construction of children as innocent and vulnerable, and hence in need of adult protection. On the other, there is a more contemporary sentimentality – a construction of children as a "media wise", active audience, possessing a kind of natural wisdom that guides their dealings with new media and technologies. Broadly speaking, it is the former view that tends to dominate the public arena, while the latter is the one increasingly espoused by the media industries themselves. Yet even within the more specialized domain of academic research, debates about children's relationships with the media are often reduced to a simple choice between these two positions: if one is false, then the other must necessarily be true.' (Buckingham, 2000: 105)

Buckingham suggests a more socio-cultural approach to children's media consumption which resists the simplistic lure of these two polarised positions. In other words, he calls for us to recognise that neither the discourse of protection from violent videogames or the postmodern view that children are naturally able to 'play' with the boundaries between reality and the virtual will do the job if we want to work out what social effects games might have. Instead we need to support (through media literacy education) young people to become participants in media through creative practice, as this is how they can become able to protect themselves.

Most media students are between the ages of 14 and 20, and if this is you, then this aspect of studying videogames will be particularly challenging because you are part of the social group that you now need to analyse. We are effectively asking you to weigh up the effects of these media texts on yourself and your peers. What often happens in this context is that students imagine an 'other' – an alternative version of a young person who might not be capable of distinguishing a game from reality, just as we sometimes assert that people under the age of 18 should not be allowed to watch certain films even though we watched them when we were 15! Nick Barham (2004) describes the 'disconnect' between games players and those that make assumptions about how the games are influencing them in this way:

'Modern entertainment fans have little respect or time for people who don't understand something making comments about the effect that it has on the people who do understand it.' (Barham, 2004: 284)

On the other hand, we cannot simply dismiss the 'discourse of concern' on the assumption that it only comes from old people who don't understand. Plenty of credible research has been carried out in this area. Consider this summary of American research conducted by paediatricians, from Gentile:

'Looking across the dozens of studies that have now been conducted on violent video games, there appear to be five major effects. Playing violent games leads to increased physiological arousal, increased aggressive thoughts, increased aggressive feelings, increased aggressive behaviors, and decreased prosocial helping. These studies include experimental studies (where it can be shown that playing violent games actually causes increases in aggression), correlational studies (where long-term relations between game play and real-world aggression can be shown), and longitudinal studies (where changes in children's aggressive behaviors can be demonstrated). For example, in a study of over 400 3rd--5th graders, those students who played more violent video games early in the school year changed to become more physically aggressive later in the school year, even after statistically controlling for sex, race, total screen time, prior aggression, and other relevant variables. Apparently practice does make perfect.' (Gentile, 2004: 1)

Taking this statement in good faith, there appears to be a great deal of scientific 'proof' that aggressive behaviour increases as a result of playing a violent game, like *Grand Theft Auto*, which we analyse in depth in Chapter 4.

But serious gamers who we spoke to in preparing this book told us a different story. They said that the more you play violent games, the more sensitive you become to the nature of the game as representational. In other words, the more violence you play, the less likely you are to be confused over what is real and what is not. This resonates with film critic Mark Kermode's argument that fans of the slasher film sub-genre are the *least* likely to be corrupted by screen gore (2007).

So who is right? The researchers that present their evidence of aggressive behaviour, decreasing social skills and the lethargy of the 'games addict', or those that see gaming as a far more complex activity with no clear-cut 'effects'?

RESEARCH STUDIES

Here we will look at four examples of research conducted into the effects of games. For each, we will firstly summarise the approach taken and the findings presented. Then we will consider the outcomes in relation to the research methods used in each case and the broader debate over the effects model.

1. **Anderson and Bushman** (2001) offer a 'meta-analytical review' of scientific research into the effects of violent videogames. Their findings include the assertions that the protagonists in high school shootings in Paducah, Jonesboro and Littleton were all habitual violent game players, which in itself is unsupported as a claim of causality. In addition, the article presents evidence that violence in games both increases aggression and decreases 'prosocial behaviour':

   'Is there a reliable assertion between exposure to violent videogames and aggression? Across 33 independent tests of the relation between videogame violence and aggression, involving 3033 participants, the average effect size was positive and significant. High video-game violence was definitely associated with heightened aggression. Indeed, this effect of violent videogames on aggression is as strong as the effect of condom use on risk of HIV infection.' (Anderson and Bushman, 2001: 357)

2. **Lt. Col. Dave Grossman** is a well-known campaigner in the United States who makes a stark connection between gaming and real aggression, as this internet report on a conference shows:

   'In the realm of video games, Grossman likens violent games to modern combat infantry simulators. In addition to desensitization, games reward mass killing as well as providing tactical training. A proper sight picture and a head shot will result in the most graphic animated response. The repetitiveness of playing a game every night makes the response automatic under the right conditions. Grossman believes that we are literally training our children to become highly efficient mass killers.' (Brian Lee, Ontario PD at http://www.killology.com/falarticle.htm, accessed 3.4.7)

Grossman cites research statistics but there is little evidence of his own empirical work.

3. **Kline and Stewart** (2005) of Simon Fraser University's Media Risk Project, have offered a range of research findings in relation to young Canadians' use of digital media and videogames in particular. Whilst their conclusions are far more subtle and complex than the authors above, their work does start from a similar premise – that there is an inevitable health risk in playing games. Consider this statement from the report of their 'Community Based Media Risk Reduction Intervention: Tune Out the Screen Challenge':

'The pilot study in North Vancouver Schools set out to make children's lives safer and healthier by reducing children's time spent watching TV, surfing the internet and playing video games. The students embraced the Tune Out challenge enthusiastically, with 64% attempting to go "cold turkey" and 28% using the controlled use approach. The researchers found that there was an 80% reduction in screen use. In the leisure time they gained, students increased both their reading and their active play.' (Kline and Stewart, 2005: 1)

Whilst few would argue that moderation in all things is a good thing and thus the findings are fairly uncontroversial, it is interesting to note that the entire research project begins from and concludes with three major and unsupported assumptions that the audience are presumably expected to accept as 'given' in each case. These are a) that a reduction in screen time inevitably serves to increase safety (which is never defined), b) that 'reading' is different to engagement with screen texts and c) that playing video games is not 'active'. As we shall see, much effects research operates in this way and whilst the findings might at first seem straightforward and worrying, it is important to scrutinise both the starting point and the context of interpretation before accepting the data wholesale.

4. An interesting example of a contextual shift is that of **Ryuta Kawashima**'s research (2001). This professor presented his theory that children playing Nintendo DS games for significant amounts of time were developing some parts of the brain at the expense of others and that this could have a negative impact on some aspects of their cognitive development. But Nintendo turned these findings around by enlisting Kawashima's expertise in producing *Brain Age* and *Big Brain Academy*, games for the DS designed specifically to train the parts of the brain previously undermined by DS play, according to Kawashima.

EVALUATING THE RESEARCH

Assessing the validity of effects research is difficult. On the one hand, there is some empirical evidence of increased aggression. But we might ask – are aggressive thoughts necessarily dangerous? Much of the research focuses on discursive outcomes – what people say, rather than actual physical behaviour. Freud's most obvious contribution to psychology was the suggestion that we all spend our lives torn between our desires in thought (what we would really like to do) and our social sense of self (what we think we should do in relation to our need to be liked and respected by others). But much of the psychological effects research could reasonably be accused of ignoring this (pretty important) detail.

Another area to follow up in order to enhance your understanding of the research itself is the laboratory context which is often used by researchers who come from a psychological approach. Looking at particular examples of such research, you might explore further the detail – how was aggression tested, in what conditions and with what kind of sample? How close is this context to real life, or how artificial, how removed? Perhaps research subjects might act more aggressively if they think that's what the researchers are looking for?

But alongside the research evidence and the 'moral panic' from the older generation, we must assess some less predictable and more specific concerns. One perhaps unusual example is the lobbying by the Sex Workers Outreach Project USA against *Grand Theft Auto*, on the grounds that in *GTA*, the rape of prostitutes is alluded to, and prostitutes are subject to murder by the player. SWOP claim that this game reinforces the idea that sex workers are 'fair game' for abuse and that their work in promoting a safe working environment for the industry is undermined by the messages of the game.

RESEARCH METHODS

Research into how media texts are 'received' has tended to be divided between *quantitative effects* research and *qualitative reception* research.

According to Jensen (2002), effects research has developed from an 'all powerful media' approach to more of a negotiated model of effects within a sense of the media as offering various forms of gratification. Meanwhile reception theories have developed from notions of 'decoding' through to ethnographic studies which (in the case of Ang's 1991 research in particular) move away from the idea of a fixed target audience towards an understanding of dispersed media consumption 'situations' and more recently to research which explores discursive boundaries between text and audience from a 'postmodern' approach. The relationship between the various research paradigms is explained by Jensen in this way:

'Quantitative audience research has been particularly successful in accounting for the "early" stages of mediated communication, such as the diffusion and consumption of each medium, and for "mid-term" effects such as recall and agenda-setting. Qualitative reception studies have proven able to supplement quantitative research by focusing on other stages of the communicative process, including the everyday contexts of media use and some of the long-term cultural implications of media.' (Jensen, 2000: 155)

PLEASURABLE DELUSIONS?

To clarify what these research terms mean in simpler terms, there has historically been a battle in this area between a view of the media as powerful (influential) and a view of the audience as powerful (making the meaning, interpreting). Originally informed by the behaviourist 'stimulus response' model of psychology, effects research moved to a more differentiated approach (different people respond differently to the same media stimulus). A further development has been more 'constructivist' work, in which the question becomes how do people interpret what they read, see or play. As we saw in the chapter on media concepts, the ludological approach to games is heavily focused on how the play experience is different in terms of the construction of meaning, to say, the act of watching a film. Buckingham (2000) suggests that the 'constructivist turn' in effects research flatters to deceive, as the behaviourist laboratory contexts and belief in rational, objectively measured data remain in place. But he also has broader concerns in relation to the conception of child development that underpins most studies in this area:

'Much of this research implicitly adopts a rationalistic notion of child development as a steady progression towards adult maturity and rationality. In the case of work on children and the media this developmental approach inevitably privileges certain kinds of judgements (particularly rational, "critical" judgements) at the expense of others. By contrast, there has been very little engagement with questions about pleasure (or displeasure) and fantasy. From this perspective, the ideal "critical" viewer is seen to be surrounded by a kind of rationalistic character armour which provides a form of protection against the pleasurable delusions promoted by the media.' (Buckingham, 2000: 111)

CHALLENGING MEDIA EFFECTS

Alongside Buckingham's critique of effects research, two other notable alternatives are the work of Barker and Petley (1998) and David Gauntlett (2005). Barker and Petley in *Ill Effects: The Media / Violence Debate* offer a simple riposte – there is no such thing as media violence and thus no effect. This claim is based on the idea that violence in the media is so varied and so contextually located that it makes no sense to talk about it in general terms. Furthermore, the authors take a political stance in opposition to the claims made by the 'effects' researchers and the campaign groups that use their findings as ammunition:

> 'Predictably, each new claim comes an imprimatur of "this time we've done it, this time we've finally proved it" – but never does an admission follow, when their claims fall apart (as they invariably do) that they were simply wrong in the first place. We have to uncover and hold up to bright daylight the unstated assumptions that come camouflaged within these claims. We have to show the ill effects of the campaigns run by the "effects" campaigners – including their effects on those whom the campaigners frequently insult and denigrate as morally debased – the people who enjoy and enthusiastically participate in the movies, TV programmes, video games or whatever that the moralists are so certain are "harmful".' (Barker and Petley, 1998: 2)

David Gauntlett's (2005) essay *Ten Things Wrong with the Media Effects Model* is fairly self-explanatory in its position. Amongst the ten problems identified, the author shares with the other writers we have discussed the view that the effects model adopts a position of superiority over media consumers (usually children), and mistakenly assumes a simplistic perception of how the media create meaning. Put simply, he argues that the effects researchers arrogantly claim that they are in the best position to understand how meaning is made, without any evidence of how they are qualified to do so. He then goes further (2007) to question not only the notion of 'the media', 'effects' and 'behaviour' as stable categories that can be pinned down, but also to move away from a notion of media audiences. In his Media Studies 2.0 essay, he makes a link between the collaborative, peer content sharing world of Web 2.0 and suggests that in the new era of media analysis:

> 'Conventional research methods are replaced – or at least supplemented – by new methods which recognise and make use of peoples' own creativity, and brush aside the outmoded notions of "receiver" audiences and elite "producers".' (Gauntlett, 2007: 4)

Two other concerns commonly expressed about the effects model (and these can both be fairly easily located in the *Telegraph* letter) are the way that people's personal tastes and dislikes of videogames get confused with research and the use of the model as a scapegoating device. The range of complex causes for antisocial behaviour, crime and various forms of 'deviance' amongst use, along with obesity, substance abuse and other health problems can more easily be blamed on videogames and other electronic media, which can be banned, censored or switched off than on the effects of global capitalism, the nature of our economy, privatisation and the increase in car ownership. All of these factors may be as or more likely to cause 'societal breakdown' but they are much harder to do anything about.

GAMES AND EDUCATION

ACTIVITY 3.5

Consider these three quotes from A Level Media students interviewed for research into videogames and learning (McDougall, 2007):

'It doesn't really feel like learning. It is fun but you are learning about it at the same time because you are in a different environment, and you are having fun but learning at the same time.'

'I play games when I have nothing better to do, which is most of the time.'

'When you are playing you don't really stop and note things down but it only really works when you stop at the end of the lesson and consolidate, when they put it into a teaching format.'

In a group, identify three assumptions / ideas that are taken for granted by these students when talking about games and learning. Why do you think these students made these assumptions?

One serious social effect of videogames relates to education. Put simply, if six- and seven-year-olds are now regularly (at least in developed, affluent areas) playing cognitively-rich games in their own time (in their 'lifeworlds' – we will come back to this idea), then arguably it is going to be even more difficult for their secondary school teachers to engage them in the traditional curriculum, which still tends to involve individual reading and writing tasks, further down the line. So education, as a whole, and individual teachers within the system are faced with a choice of three responses:

1. Ignore videogames and carry on as before (playing videogames is part of a child's private 'lifeworld', just like watching TV, and formal classroom education is not related to such hobbies).

2. Accept the powerful status of videogames in children's imaginations and create educational games that harness this power – these games are referred to as 'edutainment'.

3. Rather than create explicitly educational games (which might be poor in quality or ambience in comparison to the far more expensively produced games on the market), create new ways of teaching and learning that incorporate existing commercial videogames – for example, using videogames with a historical basis for teaching History or videogames with complex narratives to teaching English.

ACTIVITY 3.6

Activity: Talk to your teachers from other subjects than Media (the more 'traditional' the better; English and History are good ones) for their responses to the three choices listed above.

At the time of writing, many teachers seem to be adopting the second position. The *Birmingham Mail* on 28 March 2007 featured 'School Lessons by Playstation' as its headline. The article describes a pilot scheme run by Holyhead Secondary School where pupils are given PSP consoles, a project that arose from a Sony employee switching career and being recruited by the school. The paper makes a key distinction in this sentence:

> 'But there won't be any shoot em up or football games on offer – the consoles will stay in the classroom and will be initially used to help French, History and Geography lessons.' (Tony Collins, Education Correspondent, *Birmingham Mail*, 28.3.7:1)

The journalist here is maintaining what the theorist Basil Bernstein (1996) calls 'insulation' between categories – whilst the use of PSP consoles is considered a positive innovation by the paper, it is seeking to reassure readers that the devices will be used for legitimate educational practice – and playing the types of game described in the quote ('shoot em up or football games') would not do this – it would 'transgress' the insulation.

Here are some more examples of teachers using videogames in the classroom. Immersive Education, in collaboration with the Institute of Education, produced a piece of software called *Mission Maker* which allows the user to produce elements of a fantasy game and in so doing learn how games combine narrative, character and rule systems. The learning objectives here include creativity, critical thinking, literacy skills and imagination. Quoted in a *Times Educational Supplement* article, a 14-year-old user describes the experience thus:

> 'You have to write the game, the rules, develop the characters. You get to express how imaginative you can be. You have to use logic. You can't just do whatever you want.' (Quoted in Wallace, 2006: 10)

As we shall see later in this chapter, this development of imagination within logical constraints resonates with the work of educational theorist Kieran Egan who criticises mainstream education precisely for its failure to engage with this kind of creativity.

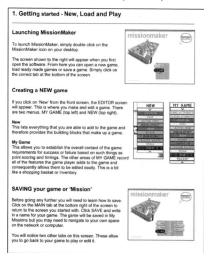

Mission Maker – engages students in new literacy and imaginative practices.

The Media Studies curriculum now features videogames as an area of study (you may well know this from first hand experience and indeed you are likely to be reading this book for that reason). But this is currently restricted to analysis of games, which does not necessarily involve playing. However some recent research into students' and teachers' experiences of this area of study raised some interesting questions about the difference between studying games and studying other forms of media, as this student articulates:

> 'Since I have started revising for the exam I have been playing the two games I am going to write about and my Mum is like – "why aren't you revising", and I say "I am revising" (laughs). But they don't understand that! Computer games are seen as something enjoyable, and it is a lot of people's pastimes. Conventionally education is not something you do for fun as a child.' (Student interview, in McDougall, 2007: 129)

A different approach is that of Tim Rylands, at Chew Magna School near Bristol, who uses an existing commercial game, *Myst*, to support literacy work, and reports that male students who were previously reluctant to write became highly engaged and produced impressive work as a result. Rylands' work differs to the other examples as he is not attempting to produce an educational game, but rather to shift his teaching strategies to incorporate a game which is already in the popular domain.

In 2005, Kurt Squire and Henry Jenkins published *Harnessing the Power of Games in Education*, describing a range of models for realising the 'pedagogic potential' of videogames. The authors see games as a good example of how 'constructivist' education works – this is where students construct knowledge on their own terms and teachers facilitate such construction (rather than simply transmitting the knowledge in a sender-receiver model). Let's consider some of the examples described in *Harnessing the Power*. *Civilisation III* is used by historians to help students make connections between periods of history, through an open ended (again, constructionist) experience in which players set their own goals in relation to 'real' historical development. *Revolution*, an edutainment game developed at MIT in collaboration with Microsoft's 'Games to Teach' project, focuses on the American revolution and allows the player to interact with a real social community through the multiplayer framework. The key here, according to the authors, is that each player has a different experience, which reflects how history is really lived. This resists the 'grand narrative' view of history which the traditional curriculum presents – the idea of 'what happened' being presented as simple fact, rather than how history was experienced and interpreted differently by different people at the time. *Environmental Detectives* offers scientific simulations through PDA devices using GPS. The player is put in the role of an environmental scientist researching a chemical spill on campus. This is called an 'augmented reality' game (virtual experience in a real physical setting) and the authors claim that such a medium allows students to engage in imaginative active play in relation to the curriculum that traditional teaching and learning cannot facilitate. More generally, they suggest that:

'Games are not simply problems or puzzles; they are microworlds, and in such environments students develop a much firmer sense of how specific social processes and practices are interwoven and how different bodies of knowledge relate to each other.' (Squire and Jenkins, 2005: 15)

ACTIVITY 3.7

Find an educational videogame and play it. Write a 200 word review, from the perspective of the player, broken down into these three areas:

a) What kinds of pleasure does the game offer you?

b) What did you learn?

c) What was the balance / relationship between playing and learning?

GAMES, LEARNING AND IMAGINATION

Staying with this theme of imagination for a while longer, the 2006 Imaginative Education conference in Vancouver, Canada brought together an international range of teachers and academics to share ideas about ways of educating the imaginative practices of students, based on Kieran Egan's theory of imaginative education:

'Imagination is too often seen as something peripheral to the core of education. In this approach imagination is at the center of education. Imagination can be the main workhorse of effective learning if we yoke it to education's central tasks. To bring knowledge to life in students' minds we must introduce it to students in the context of the human hopes, fears and passions in which it finds its fullest meaning. The best tool for doing this is the imagination.' (Egan, 2005: xii)

Several of the presenters at the conference were researching the potential of videogames to offer imaginative learning experiences. One example is Jeanne Kentel, working on the theme of 'ludology' which is explored in depth in Chapter 1. For this chapter, however, where we are considering 'effects', Kentel's work is interesting in relation to Egan's quote above because she suggests that the bodily / physical experience of videogaming can create imaginative *situated* learning, which she calls 'the recovery of the body'. If this is plausible, then taken alongside Egan's ideas, we might say that one (probably unexpected) social effect of videogames could be that students are able to learn more effectively through situated, imaginative immersion in games that can bring the curriculum to life. So games, whilst relying on mimesis – the imitation of life – allow students to 'experience' the construction of knowledge through being situated in the (virtual) subject matter of what they are learning about. Taken together with Johnson's claims that videogames are helping our thinking to get 'sharper' and the ideas about new literacies described earlier in this chapter, we could be suggesting that, contrary to the dominant view that videogames are a distraction from education, they actually have a lot to offer to teachers:

'Anyone who can draw as many people into situations related to learning as Nintendo knows something that educators ought to want to learn.' (Papert, 1994: 87)

A writer who has taken this idea further is James Paul Gee, who has written a book called *What do Videogames Have to Teach Us about Learning and Literacy* (2003). Gee lists 36 principles of 'good learning' and claims that you can find far more learning being utilised when someone plays a good videogame (he makes a distinction between rich, complex games and less intense ones for this purpose) than in the average school lesson. Gee uses the term 'connectivism' to link constructivist ideas about forming knowledge to the notion of situated learning exemplified by Kentel and Egan, above, and concludes that:

'The theories of learning one would infer from looking at schools today comport very poorly with the theory of learning in good videogames. If the principles of learning in good videogames are good, then better theories of learning are embedded in the videogames many children play than in the schools they attend.' (Gee, 2003: 7)

In 2004, the Learning and Skills Development Agency produced a report for teachers in England on the possible uses of videogames in education. Here, unlike Gee's suggestions, the LSDA is interested in educational games (or edutainment). Whilst recognising the budgetary limitations of educational games design and the risk therefore of edutainment games failing to engage young people, the authors suggest that:

'There is a strong case for games to incorporate creative tools, giving the learner control. This can extend to allowing them to enhance the game or create new games. It is true that few learners may want or feel able to take up such options and that even if they do so the results may be unsatisfactory. Nevertheless it is vital to encourage aspiration in learning with at risk students in particular. It would be beneficial for the game to afford opportunities for players to personalise the medium, thereby allowing them to key into their lifelong learning experience. This is important because games should not just relate to the curriculum, but also to youth culture and learning styles.' (Mitchell and Savill-Smith, 2004: 60)

If this can be taken on board, then we can suggest that another social effect of videogames might be the 'handing over' of control of learning to students and even a connecting of the curriculum to the broader culture of students –what we call their 'lifeworld'. By the time this book is published, the British Government commissioned *Byron Review* of young people's digital media consumption will be available. The reader is strongly advised to read this review alongside this chapter, and to try to 'locate' the outcomes in the theoretical contexts we have explored.

ACTIVITY 3.8 – THE SOCIAL EFFECTS OF GRAND THEFT AUTO

In this book we are using *Grand Theft Auto* as a case study for all of our analytical approaches to videogames. In relation to effects, *GTA* is one of the most controversial games ever produced.

In March 2005 Take Two Interactive, Sony and Wal-Mart, Gamespot were all sued in Alabama by the parents of a murdered police officer. The basis of their lawsuit was their belief that 18-year-old Devin Moore had shot three police officers as a direct result of playing *Grand Theft Auto*, and thus the producers and retailers of the game that had led him to be influenced in this way were culpable.

The main piece of evidence to support this allegation was the claim that Moore had said 'Life is like a videogame. Everybody's got to die some time' on his arrest. One of the injured officers asked this question to the designers and promoters of *GTA* – 'Why do you make games that target people that are there to protect us, police officers, people that we look up to, why do you want to market a game that gives people the thoughts of thinking it's OK to shoot police officers? Why do you want to do that?' (Source: www.cbsnews.com/stories/2005/03/04/ 60minutes)

For a synoptic application of our work on social effects to *Grand Theft Auto*, do the following:

a) Play *Grand Theft Auto* as intensively as you can for a week.

b) Design a psychological experiment to test your own responses to the game's violent content.

c) Get together with two other students who have done the same thing and compare notes – have you all used the same methods?

d) Discuss – is it possible to design a psychological experiment on yourself?

e) Set up a blog or a wiki with other students to discuss the Alabama case described above in the context of your own responses to playing *Grand Theft Auto*.

f) Conduct ethnographic reception research with a cross section of your local community to gauge their situated responses to *Grand Theft Auto* – you may decide that the research subjects should play the game or they might view game play sequences or trailers that you have prepared or downloaded from the internet. Depending on your resources, you may wish to conduct this research online using a video podcast or MP4 distribution. Share your findings on the blog / wiki you set up in (e).

g) Set up a new thread on the blog to discuss the potential for *GTA* to be used for educational purposes. For this thread, extend the blog / wiki community to include teachers.

h) If you are following an essay-based academic course, use the material you have collected so far to answer this question in 1000 words: **To what extent do videogames have tangible social effects?**

4. *GRAND THEFT AUTO*: PUBLIC ENEMY NUMBER 1?

MISSION BRIEFING

 Grand Theft Auto – *brain pollutant?*

In this chapter, all the ideas and concepts explored so far will be used to explore the *Grand Theft Auto* (*GTA*) series, or franchise, of games. Firstly, we will document the various games that make up the series, exploring the variety of features they have included to bring to life how the games have changed and developed as game technology – both on the development side and the playing side – has changed and developed. This survey of the series will then enable a thorough analysis of what the *GTA* games are doing and saying, working through some of the major perspectives, theories and concepts in Media Studies and the new academic field of Game Studies.

The analysis of the *GTA* game series will explore what game genres the games can be classified as 'belonging' to and trace the cultural ancestors of the *GTA* games through looking at the influence of other media and other media texts on the franchise. Notably, this will mean exploring the gangster film genre and its undeniable influence on the games and the influence of films such as *Scarface* (1983) and television programmes such as *Miami Vice* on the style and iconography of the games – particularly *Vice City* and *Vice City Stories*. Through exploring the concepts surrounding postmodernism and the media, the view that the *GTA* games are sophisticated, postmodern texts will be advanced.

The third section will put the *GTA* series on trial – *GTA* stands charged with corrupting the minds of its players through its gratuitous violence, sexism, racism and glamourisation of gangsterism and criminality. This section will also tackle the controversial debate of the influence of videogames on game players, and tackle the age-old debate within Media Studies about how media violence does or doesn't lead to real violence.

SHAKE YOUR MONEY MAKER — THE *GTA* FRANCHISE AND ROCKSTAR GAMES

The *GTA* franchise – game features and developments

 Over a decade of mindless mayhem?

The expression 'from little acorns do mighty oak trees grow' is readily applicable to the *GTA* series. At the time of writing in early 2008, the series or franchise is now just over ten years old, with the latest addition to the *GTA* family in the shape of *GTA 4* released in April 2008. The strength of the series is demonstrated through comparison to other videogame series. There are very few game series which have enjoyed the kind of 'staying power' that the *GTA* games have had with their audiences – *Lara Croft*, *Resident Evil*, *Medal of Honor* are the only game series which have stood the test of time as well as *GTA*. Looking at other media, this longevity seems even more remarkable. In the music industry, not many artists get to ten years in the music business still enjoying good sales for CDs and concert tickets – there are many more short-lived music careers than long ones, more Gareth Gates than Rolling Stones.

Grand Theft Auto

A good way of starting to think about how the *GTA series* has changed and evolved is to start at the beginning and explore some of the promotional blurb put out to market *GTA*. On the packaging for the game itself, the manufacturer's description of the game runs as follows:

'Experience for yourself every classic car ever seen. Race at breakneck speed through a living city, out-running and outwitting rival gang members, mercenaries, hired killers and an entire force. Drive dozens of varied vehicles around three of America's toughest cities. Only the best tame the fastest cars.'

Title	Platform	Year of release
GTA	PS1	1997
	PC	1997
	Game Boy Color (GBC)	1999
GTA 2	PS1	1999
	PC	1999
	GBC	2000
GTA: London	PS1	2003
GTA 3	PS2	2001
	XBox	2002
	PC	2002
GTA: Vice City	PS2	2001
	XBox	2003
	PC	2003
GTA: San Andreas	PS2	2004
	XBox	2005
	PC	2005
GTA: Liberty City Stories	PSP	2005
GTA: Vice City Stories	PSP	2006
	PS2	2007
GTA 4	PS3	2008
	XBox 360	2008

(Source: Kerr, A., 'Spilling Hot Coffee?', in Garrelts, N., 2006)

Considering that the GTA series has become synonymous with the media violence debate (which is explored later in the GTA 'in the Dock' section of chapter 4), it is interesting to note that GTA is here being marketed more as a racing game rather than one where the narrative structure and objectives of the game require the player to be a career criminal. At this early stage in its gestation, GTA is more reminiscent of The Fast and the Furious (2001) than Scarface (1983), which the series came to resemble with GTA: Vice City.

This emphasis on GTA as a car racing game is also to be found in the 'product features' listed on the GTA page on the Amazon site, mentioning features such as 'over 6000km of freeways, back streets, roads, alleyways and dead ends, ...no fixed track'.

Significant in their omission from these promotional texts are other key facets of the GTA experience; for example, the interpolation of the player into the criminal world, the RPG (role playing game) side to GTA and the beat 'em up elements of the game, too – these would become more heavily featured as the series progressed.

Grand Theft Auto 2

Regardless of media and product, when releasing any kind of sequel to a prior text – whether that media text is a film, CD or videogame – in order to persuade people to buy the new product, media institutions need to convince prospective buyers that the new product does indeed offer you something new and different to what you already have. This is very much the case for *GTA 2*. This writer's memories of playing *GTA* and *GTA 2* was that I couldn't much distinguish between them – the type of narrative structure present in both games was identical and the style of game design was near identical too. However, the available promotional literature for the games is very different. As noted above, for *GTA* the marketing focused on the car racing aspects of *GTA*; the promotional material for *GTA 2* notes the following features of the game – 'prove your criminal instincts to warring gangs, carjack innocent victims, assassinate rivals, steal drug shipments'. Additionally, the tagline for the game, again featuring on the packaging was 'Go anywhere. Steal anything. Jack anyone.'

From reading these diverse approaches alone, it would be easy to come to the conclusion that *GTA* and *GTA 2* were very different types of game, but the reality of playing the game suggests that this was not so. For instance, carjacking was an integral part of *GTA* – getting around Liberty City by foot is a boring and slow business! Whilst set in different fictionalised cities, the reality of the playing experience suggests that there was little difference between *GTA* and *2* – a triumph of marketing over game design.

GTA: London

One for the Brits, but similar to *GTA 2*, essentially treading water and offering game players a pretty similar game experience to what they would have already enjoyed with *GTA* and *2*. A reviewer on the Amazon site notes that '*GTA: London* seems a little lacklustre, half-hearted…' (http://www.amazon.co.uk/Grand-Theft-Auto-London-Budget/dp/B000059LRA/ref=pd_sim_vg_h__3_img/203-3711143-1791102?ie=UTF8&qid=1184539621&sr=8-21). One might suspect that this was one game produced rather opportunistically or perhaps to act as a stopgap before *GTA 3*. Apart from the different and true to life area and street names, visually there isn't much to pick this game out from what came before.

GTA 3

The great leap forward from 2D to 3D, from top-down to immersive gameworld

After the limited momentum the series demonstrated in *GTA 2* and *GTA: London*, the series took a massive leap forward with the arrival of *GTA 3*. The single biggest reason for this was the innovative and timely shift from 2D to 3D game play. Not surprisingly, this shift always marks the mutation of the series from PS1 and consoles and operating systems of the 5th generation of consoles (see Chapter 2 for further details) to the PS2 and the 6th generation of consoles, and what was then known as 'next generation'. *GTA 3* made its debut on the PS2 in 2001 being followed in 2002 by versions, or 'ports', for the XBox and PC in 2002 (the reason for the time delay due to the Rockstar / Take Two Interactive exclusivity deal with Sony that the *GTA* games would first appear on the PS2 ('Spilling Hot Coffee?', Kerr, A. in Garrelts, N., 2006).

In terms of overall objectives and game narrative, nothing has really changed from *GTA*, but the style of this game ushered the series into the 'stadium rock' league of videogames because of the shift from 2D and the top-down zooming functionality of the early games to 3D and therefore allowing far more engagement and empathy. *GTA* had become big business and was here to stay.

The importance of the success of *GTA 3* for both the series and the PS2 is to be noted. This can be seen in this extract from an Amazon review posted by 'CarlosPeterGaryJohn' who stated, 'Looking back this game transformed the PS2…It is the most revolutionary, original and enjoyable game made…this made the PS2 what it is' (http://www.amazon. co.uk/Grand-Theft-Auto-III-PS2/dp/B00005NZ38/ref=pd_sim_vg_h__4_img/203-3711143-1791102?ie=UTF8&qid=1184539621&sr=8-21).

This review brings to light an important part of the videogame industry – the symbiosis between hardware (games consoles) manufacturers and software (games) manufacturers. Both sets of institutions depend on each other for continued critical and commercial success – for consoles such as the PS2 to work commercially for Sony, they need games which can pull big audiences and spread positive word-of-mouth. Similarly, media institutions such as Rockstar, the publishers of the *GTA* series, need good and improving hardware if they are to be able to develop their products.

GTA: Vice City

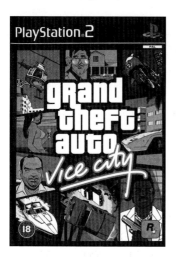

With the huge success of *GTA 3* and the move from 2D top-down style game play to 3D and a more immersive gameworld, Rockstar didn't need to do much tinkering with what had now become a very successful formula. With *Vice City*, the designers' mantra seems to have been that 'more is more' – so in *Vice City*, the basic operation of the game remains the same as *GTA 3* (if it ain't broke, don't fix it). The key difference this time was the shift of location – moving away from Liberty City (alias New York City) to Vice City (alias Miami). This relocation to a new city also mirrors the success and trend of the *CSI* franchise in television – *CSI* is based in Las Vegas and the spin-off programmes have been *CSI: New York* and *CSI: Miami*. The *CSI* family, or franchise, of programmes essentially share the same formula of a group of detectives who painstakingly solve cases through working the forensic evidence. This copying of a successful formula is exactly what occurred with the release of *GTA: Vice City* – this isn't so much a sequel to *GTA 3* but a spin-off from it. Arguably, this is hinted at in the name of the game – this isn't *GTA 4* in the same way that *GTA: London* wasn't *GTA 2* but rather a spin-off from the original *GTA*.

The commercial success of *GTA 3* (the game stayed in the game charts for over a year following it's release) paved the way for a bigger game development budget for *Vice City* – the game boasts a bigger explorable city, claiming that *Vice City* is 'over twice the size of Liberty City and double its missions'. This would mean more game development time which necessitates more money being spent plus the artists providing voice-overs for the game's characters were starting to step up a notch in reputation. In *Vice City* the gamer plays the character of Tommy Vercetti, voiced by Ray Liotta, who is most well known for his role in *Goodfellas* (1990), one of the finest entries in the gangster film genre. This is a significant advance from the original *GTA*, where the gamer has the option of playing a character called 'Travis', a reference to Travis Bickle from the New York-set *Taxi Driver* (1976). But this Travis bore no physical resemblance to Bickle and neither was the character voiced by Robert De Niro, who played Travis Bickle – these are the types of differences in scale that commercial success with the previous games afforded plus the differences that can be achieved in game development with the progression from designing PS1 and the 5th generation of consoles to PS2 and the 6th generation. These design innovations due to more sophisticated game development hardware and game playing hardware (in the shape of the PS2) enabled more spectator involvement – or immersion – in the game.

In addition to Ray Liotta, the game also featured voice-overs by notable Hollywood names such as Tom Sizemore, Dennis Hopper, Burt Reynolds and Philip Michael Thomas, who played Tubbs in the TV series *Miami Vice*. The ability of videogames such as *Vice City* to attract well-known actors shows how videogames were now starting to make a significant mark on popular culture.

Additionally, *Vice City* also boasts more character moves, greater intelligence with the characters you encounter on the streets – when you attempt a carjacking in *Vice City* you have to be ready for a feisty driver – unlike the meek and mild car drivers of the original *GTA* who would simply run away as soon as you opened their car door.

With an eye on expanding the target audience for the series, *Vice City* is set in the 1980s and sports an 80s jukebox to match, featuring 80s classics such as Frankie Goes To Hollywood's 'Two Tribes' and Michael Jackson's 'Wanna Be Startin' Somethin', thus broadening the appeal to a slightly older audience in addition to teenagers, hard-core gamers and a 20-something audience. This also helped the game to keep pace with the ever widening console owning population – these things aren't just owned by 'kids' but by adults of a variety of ages, similar to how the internet has never simply been a youth dominated medium.

GTA: Liberty City Stories

Whilst *Liberty City Stories* has subsequently become available across different gaming platforms, the original release of this game was on Sony PSP – and was to be used as one of the main driver of sales of this new step forward in gaming. The portable console with PS2 standard graphics, differentiated itself from the chain of Nintendo Game Boy products, which have never boasted especially good graphics capabilities.

Rockstar arguably played it conservatively by going back to Liberty City, which allowed it to use its existing game development engine and copy across the style of design from *GTA 3*. In the same way that *Vice City* is probably more accurately described as a spin-off rather than a sequel to *GTA 3*, this is the case for *Liberty City Stories*. Perhaps the real point of the publication of this game was to establish the franchise on PSP, enabling Sony to push its new console with an established game brand name and enabling Rockstar to tread water slightly and start focusing on game development for what was then the 'next generation' for consoles in the shape of PS3 and XBox 360, and what is now the current generation of consoles with the XBox 360 and PS3.

GTA: San Andreas

The great push west

Again taking the 'more is more' approach, *GTA: San Andreas* takes a leaf out of *Vice City*'s book, and doesn't just provide the player a bigger city to play in, but a whole state featuring three cities based on Los Angeles, San Francisco and Las Vegas. The sheer size of the game and the wealth of acting talent providing voice-overs – such as Ice-T, Samuel L. Jackson, Chris Penn and the near legendary Peter Fonda (who wrote and starred in the subversive film about American 'civilisation' in *Easy Rider* in 1969 which ran literally and metaphorically contrary to the mythology sown in the Western genre) – reinforce the point made earlier about the ever deeper connections between videogames and other spheres of popular culture. The effects of the financial success of the franchise were now really being felt. This game improves on *Vice City* with a greater range of transportation available, but arguably, you have a broadly similar game to *Vice City* except on a bigger scale.

With the release of *San Andreas*, the sales mushroomed – this game selling over 5 million copies in 2 months alone in the United States (www.wired.com/gaming/gamingreviews/news/2007/03/FF_160_rockstar, accessed on 21/5/07).

GTA: Vice City Stories

In the same way that *Liberty City Stories* borrowed its graphics engine and narrative from *GTA 3* and as such can be viewed as *GTA 3*'s little brother, *Vice City Stories* has a sibling relationship with *Vice City* and *San Andreas*. This game borrows some of the additional character functionality introduced in *San Andreas* – such as being able to swim. One thing that *Liberty City Stories* did bring back was multiplayer options, which had faded away from the series very early on. This is possibly recognition of the growing size of MMPORGs such as *World of Warcraft* and *Second Life*, and a realisation that console games would need to offer greater multiplayer functionality as online gaming through XBox Live took off. However, while the games keep on getting bigger and slicker, the basic narrative and mode of playing have remained uniform throughout the series – the gamer is pitched into a world where criminal enterprise is what sees you through.

Grand Theft Auto IV

Time for a spot of crystal ball gazing! At the time of writing, it is still some months away from the release of *GTA IV*, due to be released simultaneously on XBox 360 and PS3 in spring 2008. The simultaneous release on PS3 and XBox 360 is a first for the series, as the titles have been PlayStation oriented in the first instance – releases have come first for the PS consoles and then have been 'ported' or converted for other platforms such as the XBox or PSP, as described earlier in this chapter. This possibly indicates that Rockstar is not looking to favour either Microsoft or Sony until the battle for dominance between the PS3 and XBox 360 is clearer cut. Given Sony's pre-eminent standing in the console market prior to the launches of the XBox 360 and Nintendo's Wii, this shows how fluid and dynamic the console and videogame market is. In keeping with the other major evolutions in the series, *GTA IV* marks a return to the mean streets of *Liberty City*. However, in a break away from pop-culture savvy, recent *GTA* games, in *GTA IV* you are playing an eastern European immigrant criminal, Niko Bellic. Of course, what this also heralds is a return to the central tenets of the gangster genre in popular media forms – as this game, if played successfully, will be a traditional, conventional 'rags to riches' gangster story. The available (go to www.rockstargames.com for a look) online trailers documents this return to Liberty City – as some of the architecture features the Statue of Liberty, the Empire State Building and the Brooklyn Bridge – all icons of New York. In addition to the return to Liberty City, the emerging news on *GTA IV* also suggests something of a back to basics approach – moving on from the heavy use of film actors to provide voice-overs and to focus more intently on the game itself rather than the game as vehicle for spotting postmodern intertextual references.

ACTIVITY 4.1

Task – Construct a family tree of the *GTA* franchise.

Objective – To consolidate your knowledge and understanding of the history of the franchise and of the developments in game development and game features.

What to do – Starting with *GTA* at the top of the tree and finishing with *GTA IV* at the bottom of the tree, construct a family tree of the franchise, working out what the 'parent' games are – the ones which push the franchise forward in terms of characters, game features and general gameplay and what the 'sibling' games are. Use Google (www.google.com) to search for images to help you in this task.

ROCKSTAR GAMES

Frequent reference has already been made to Rockstar and Rockstar Games. For readers new to game culture this name may not mean very much – the purpose of this section is to provide an overview of who Rockstar Games is, what it does and speculate on why it does it.

Who are Rockstar Games?

In common with other institutions operating in other media, Rockstar Games are not just one monolithic enterprise but it is actually composed of a number of groups – namely, Rockstar Japan, Rockstar Leeds, Rockstar Lincoln, Rockstar London, Rockstar North, Rockstar San Diego, Rockstar Toronto and Rockstar Vancouver. The Rockstar Games group is in turn owned by another video game publisher, Take Two Interactive, which is based in the United States. Simply reading through the names of the different Rockstar studios gives the reader a very good idea of the international dimension of game development, and also echoes the structure of ownership and control to be found in other media industries and media institutions. What is also very noticeable about the list of Rockstar studios is how many of them are British based – four out of eight studios are based in Britain. This is a testament to the historically strong skills of British game developers and designers, dating back to the heyday of the old Atari 2600, the Spectrum and the Commodore 64 in the 1980s (see Chapter 2 for further details). However, while much of Rockstar Games' product development is occurring in the UK, ultimately the profits flow back across the Atlantic to Take Two Interactive, the owners of Rockstar, based in New York. Again, this trend echoes ownership and control structures in other media industries and institutions – such as cinema chains in Britain, where the owners of chains such as Cineworld, Odeon, Vue and Showcase Cinemas are all headquartered in the US.

Each different Rockstar Games studio works on different projects. For example, the controversial game *Manhunt 2* was produced by Rockstar London. However the *GTA* series has been developed by what is now Rockstar North, formerly DMA Games (whose logo can be found on *GTA* games up until *GTA 3*) which is based in Edinburgh. While the *GTA* series has always been based in American cities real or imagined (see the above section for full details of settings for the various games), the development work has been done in the UK – another 'fact of life' in the trans-national globalised media world. Again, in other media industries and institutions it is common practice for work to be done in a place entirely not relating to its setting – the D-Day landing beach sequence in *Saving Private Ryan*, set on the beaches of Normandy, France, was filmed on the beaches of Co. Wexford, Ireland.

What does Rockstar Games do?

While it's not necessary here to itemise each game that Rockstar has produced, it's worth taking note that Rockstar has not simply been working on *GTA* games for the past 10 years or more. Undoubtedly the huge success of the franchise, and particularly games such as *GTA 3*, *Vice City* and *San Andreas* have been money spinners for the company, but the company has had notable commercial successes with games such as *Bully* (which also stirred up some notoriety in some sections of the media for its violence, exactly as the *GTA* series has done). Other notable successes have been *Manhunt*, *Max Payne* and *Max Payne 2*, *State of Emergency* and *Oni*. Like any savvy media producer in any highly competitive media industry, Rockstar Games does not rely entirely on one product (such as the *GTA* series) to make all of its money, it ventures into different game genres and playing styles in order to attract different types of audience to its games. By limiting its dependency on the *GTA* franchise, Rockstar is engaging in smart business practice and limiting its risk – in exactly the same way record labels limit theirs by having a variety of different types of music artist under contract to them. For example, EMI, one of the 'big 4' record labels, has a diverse range of artists such as Robbie Williams, Iron Maiden, Pink Floyd, Starsailor and Corinne Bailey Rae under contract – this is part of the process of not being over-reliant on one type of artist or one genre of music, as tastes in music shift with different musical fashions, as is the case with videogames.

Why does Rockstar keep producing *GTA* games? ('Everything counts in large amounts')

With so many *GTA* games having been produced since 1997 (nearly one per year), people new to Media Studies might wonder what attraction there would be for Rockstar Games to keep producing *GTA* games – given the big similarities that exist over the series as pointed out in the section above. What needs to be borne in mind is that the videogame industry is a multi-million dollar industry. On the success or failure of videogames, the fate of whole companies can rest – a far cry from the infancy of the gaming industry in the 70s and 80s where it was not uncommon for games publishers, or 'software houses' as they were then known, to be essentially one-person armies and run part-time alongside studying or working in other occupations.

ACTIVITY 4.2

Task – What is the latest news on Rockstar Games?

Objective – To bring up-to-date your knowledge about what projects Rockstar Games is currently involved in promoting and how its work is perceived about by a range of commentators on videogames.

What to do:

Part 1 – What projects is Rockstar Games currently promoting? Go to www.rockstargames. com and explore.

Firstly, try to work out who you think the target audience is – consider age, gender, social class.

Next, with the information you have and your ideas about target audience in mind, list reasons why Rockstar is producing these games – taking each game in turn.

Part 2 – What do various commentators think about the games that Rockstar Games produces?

Using google.com as your starting point run searches on each of the game titles that you have noted down from Part 1 and note down the key points about what other commentators say about the games – this will draw you into the thorny issue of the effects of games, which features later in this chapter and will cover some of the areas that the earlier chapter on the effects of games covered.

For Marxists, the logic behind every action in a capitalist, money-oriented society is down to economics, and economics is about money – this is known as the base-superstructure model. This base-superstructure model can be used to explain why Rockstar keeps on producing *GTA* games – because they keep selling and selling in big numbers. For as long as *GTA* games keep selling huge quantities, Rockstar will keep producing them. The statistics on sales of the *GTA* games tell their own tale – 50 million *GTA* games sold, which has generated over $1 billion in revenue (www.wired.com/gaming/gamingreviews/news/2007/03/FF_160_rockstar, accessed on 21/5/07). Indeed, it has been argued that *GTA 3* is the biggest selling game of all time (www.bbc.co.uk/dna/collective/A867099 accessed on 23/5/07).

GTA – WHO ARE YOU? CLASSIFICATION, IDENTIFICATION AND CONSIDERING THE GTA GAMES AS POSTMODERN TEXTS

Now that the ancestry of the *GTA* series has been established, it is time to turn our attention to applying some media concepts and media theory to establish what kind of games the *GTA* games are. Following this process of classification, the focus will then turn to a consideration of the *GTA* games as postmodern texts.

Classification

In any sphere of life, in any media form, we always attempt to classify. Classifying people or objects or media texts works on a process of similarity and dissimilarity. For example, when walking down the street, if you were to see someone from a distance wearing a dress you might well presume that person is a girl or woman. If you were to make this classifying decision, you would be analysing that person and placing them within a stream of people, and how you expect males and females to dress. However, it may turn out that that person was not a female but instead a male – after all, there are no iron laws that dictate that only females can wear dresses. All we have are cultural norms.

The process of classification is never a pure or an easy one, but it's a process with which we engage all the time and this is a way of helping to make sense, meaning and order out of what would otherwise be a world of chaos. We apply the same type of logic when interacting with media texts. We classify films by thinking of their similarities and dissimilarities – we label films as 'action films' because the characters, situations and narrative remind us of other films we have seen which are also labelled 'action films'. Accordingly we know that something is not an action film when it bears little similarity to what we expect of an action film and instead we apply some other label – 'romantic comedy', 'musical', 'gangster' or 'horror'. We do exactly the same when listening to music, when watching television programmes, when listening to radio programmes – we make quick and usually accurate judgements about what type, or genre, of product it is and whether or not this product is for us, assessing if we are part of the target audience.

95

Identifying genre

In order to decipher what genre, or genres, the *GTA* games can be labelled as, some concepts from Film Studies will be utilised. When setting about the process of classifying a film as belonging to one genre or another there is an 'iron triangle' which can be used to start the process of deciphering and labelling, but it should be emphasised that this is only intended as a starting point and there are other issues and questions that when interrogating the genre of any media text you may also wish to consider. This iron triangle consists of examining three things – iconography, time and location. Briefly put, iconography (or *mise-en-scène*) is settings, costumes, props. When considering time, we are thinking about time periods – this could be centuries, (e.g. twentieth century), or decades (e.g. 1840s) or individual days (e.g. 11 September 2001). Finally, analysing location is considering where a text is set – town, region and country, as appropriate to the text.

Arguably, the *GTA* games can have at least three genre labels readily applied to them – the RPG (role playing game), car racing game and the beat 'em up. It is possible to argue that other genres could also be applied, but these three will be sufficient for this examination.

GTA as RPG

The conventions of RPG were set before RPGs started to be produced for computer games and videogames. The base element of any RPG is that there is a character which the player inhabits within the game. In *GTA*, the gamer 'plays' the character of 'Travis', while in *Vice City Stories* the gamer 'plays' the character of 'Vic Vance'.

As the series has progressed, a sharper sense of characterisation has emerged – in *GTA* you know very little about your chosen character other than his name. When playing as 'Vic Vance' in *Vice City Stories* you know a great deal about the character – you can learn his back-story from the material provided with the game and from the *Vice City Stories* strategy book (Vance is a former corporal in the army). There are a great many RPG videogames, or perhaps more accurately, videogames with an RPG element – *Lord of the Rings*, *Spider-Man*, the *Medal of Honor* series, the *FIFA* series of football games and many more. What all of these games have in common – and therefore forming one of the conventions of the RPG genre – is that they offer the player a character or a range of characters and at the moment you start playing the game, you metaphorically step into their shoes and you make the game, and the game makes you, behave in certain ways.

Applying this conceptual work to playing *GTA: Vice City*, at the moment that I start playing the game, I step into the role of Tommy Vercetti. As part of the process of playing *Vice City*, in the role of Tommy Vercetti, I start the game with no money, no transport and no weapons but with a head full of revenge as I have been framed. Accordingly, the way in which I choose to play or perform the role of Tommy Vercetti is bound by the rules of the gameworld and the narrative of the game over which I, as a player, have no control. I could make the choice not to engage in any criminal activity whatsoever and be a law abiding citizen. However, if I were to do that I would spend my entire time running about *Vice City* on foot, not being able to do anything other than run. This would be a very boring game to play. To make any progress within the game and to be able to enjoy the process of playing the game, I, as Tommy Vercetti, must break the law – by carrying out a carjacking I can get a mode of transportation which is quick and pleasant but would otherwise be unavailable to me. Plus, I get the opportunity to listen to a wide variety of 'classic' 80s music. If I want money I must physically assault a tourist or a prostitute – I can only get money by breaking the law. Thus, I am fully entering into playing the role as Tommy Vercetti. Therefore, the *GTA* games can be labelled as RPG games.

GTA as car racing / driving game

As discussed earlier, much of the promotional material around the marketing of *GTA* stressed the attraction of racing cars around a city modelled on New York, thereby adding something different and new to the racing genre – offering the player a racing game experience a lot different to the more conventional racing game experience provided by games such as the *Out Run* series. Car racing games, regardless of their degree of technical polish – whether they have been developed for the Atari 2600 or for the PS3 – have always been about putting the game player in the position of the driver of a car (be it a racing car or a street car) and allowing you to have fun driving it around the track. This writer first experienced the car racing genre when playing the coin-operated arcade version of Sega's *Out Run* – this game placed the player into the role of a driver of a car and your objective was simple – drive as fast as you can and beat the clock. These basic conventions of the racing game have been virtually unmodified since those days of playing in arcades in the mid 1980s. This element of the racing game makes it through to the various *GTA* formats virtually unscathed – one of your tasks in any of the *GTA* games is to drive unfamiliar and difficult to control cars on unfamiliar streets or racing circuits. Probably the biggest difference between the racing game element of the *GTA* series compared to dedicated racing games such as those named above is that you can swap and change cars so long as you are able to carry out successful carjackings without interference from the police! Thus, in addition to conceptualising *GTA* games as RPGs, they are car racing games too.

GTA as beat 'em up

Like the RPG and racing game genre, the beat 'em up game genre is one of long-standing popularity within game culture. The staple element of any beat 'em up game is having a range of characters for your character to …beat up. This writer first introduced himself to the beat 'em up genre with a game called *International Karate* (*IK*) which was originally

*Judging by the number of sales of the games and the number of websites that have some connection to the game – a Google search on the words 'grand theft auto' returns over 8 million hits.

produced for the Commodore 64 in 1987.

The narrative shape of *IK* was beautifully simplistic – your character was presented with another character for you to beat up and this process carried on until you had beaten up a lot of people. Compared to the game consoles of the current gaming generation, the Commodore 64 had seriously limited graphic capabilities, so *IK* was a rather static game – your character could move around from left to right in the foreground of the game's environment but nowhere else. As gaming technology has developed, characters have had greater freedom to explore the environment of the *GTA* games, but even in *GTA*, your character had considerable freedom to run around… beating people up.

Perhaps you don't fancy driving around Liberty City in *GTA* or London in *GTA: London* – you don't have to if you really don't want to. There has always been a certain amount of freedom to the narrative structure of the *GTA* games – instead you could terrorise them by foot, giving you more opportunities to viciously attack unsuspecting pedestrians. As the *GTA* series has developed, the process of beating up an innocent pedestrian has grown yet more rewarding – in the later games you can make them bleed and by repeatedly hitting them you can make them bleed copiously! This is a sign of greater artificial intelligence being applied due to the more sophisticated games engine used for development. However, the beat 'em up aspect of the game remains nearly identical to the mode of playing and type of pleasure to be gained from playing games like *IK* many moons ago. So, again, another genre label can be appropriately applied.

As the *GTA* games fit so comfortably within a variety of different game genres, the logical conclusion is to say that the games of the *GTA* game series are a generic hybrid. The producers have very successfully* crafted a series of games which appeal to a great many people criss-crossing many demographic boundaries and target audiences.

ACTIVITY 4.3

Task – Genre classification exercise.

Objective – To development your understanding in this section about identification of generic types and how to classify games as belonging to a genre or variety of genres.

What to do – Pick between 3 – 5 videogames with which you are familiar (the titles of the games from Activity 4.2 or the other games mentioned in earlier chapters would be suitable). For each game think through the narrative structure of the game, how you control your avatar and general aspects of how the gameplay 'handles'. Then work out how the game fits into different genre 'boxes' by thinking about they key reference points of time, location, iconography and about how you actually play the game. Use the section above as a model from which to work out your ideas and answers.

Homage or Grand Theft? *GTA* as postmodern text

Postmodernism is defined and described in a range of different ways. One of the ways sociologist and popular culture theorist Dominic Strinati defines postmodernism is in 'the breakdown of the distinction between art and popular culture' (Strinati, 1995: 225). On the website www.bbc.co.uk/dna/collective/A867099 (accessed on 23/5/07), this kind of connection or blurring between the lines of art and popular culture is alluded to with regard to *Vice City* because of its incorporation of many well-known actors working as voice artists in the game – this is one sure sign that these games are postmodern texts.

Before examining how it is possible to conceptualise the *GTA* series as a series of increasingly sophisticated postmodern texts, it is worthwhile exploring two of the terms that will be used in this section.

Bricolage – A combination of different elements brought together to make something new. For example, the film *The Blair Witch Project* (1999) is one example of bricolage in action. What the producers have done is to fuse elements of different film genres together: the horror film with the haunted house; the documentary film with the shaky handheld camerawork; the teen movie with the teenagers who go away on a holiday or expedition. Fusing these generic elements together facilitated something new and different which had a positive impact with film audiences as its runaway commercial and critical success testifies.

Intertextuality – The process of consciously referencing to other texts within a text to generate a response in the reader of the text. For example, the children's television programme *Balamory* (2002–05) regularly focused on the character of PC Plum when something or someone needs to be found. When PC Plum is given a mission to find something, there are two intertextual references to other media texts which are designed for adults watching with their children to enjoy. The reference comes through a close-up on the feet of PC Plum and another character walking across a cobbled street – this directly echoes the end credit sequence in the police serial *The Bill*. In addition to that visual reference to a television programme, there is one for rock music fans too – when PC Plum bursts into song, a basic effect is used to 'copy and paste' faces around the screen, in the same style as was done for the music video for 'Bohemian Rhapsody' by Queen in 1975. Thus, this rich postmodern text is offering something for audiences of a variety of ages and interests – in exactly the same way as the postmodern references within the *GTA* games do, although the sheer size, complexity and number of *GTA* games mean it is not possible to analyse all aspects of the *GTA* series to sift for evidence of the texts of aspects of postmodernism. When intertextual references are self-consciously used, these are also known as *homages*.

Firstly, let's consider the locations of the games. To recap, Liberty City is based on New York City, Vice City is based on Miami, Los Santos is based on Los Angeles, San Fierro is based on San Francisco, Las Venturas is based on Las Vegas and last but not least London

*For further detail on the roots of the gangster genre, watch Martin Scorsese's great documentary on the history of film, 'A Personal Journey with Martin Scorsese through American Movies' (BFI TV, 1995).

is based on… London. The choices made by the games' developers to base the games in these cities are significant if we consider the roots of the gangster genre in film and the conventional settings for gangster films.

The settings of the gangster genre have predominantly been the big cities to be found on the east and west coasts of America. When it comes to British gangster films, the usual setting is London. The first gangster films were set in New York so it was at least apt that the first *GTA* was set in a facsimile New York. For the gangster film genre the big cities have been the natural places to locate their texts, by virtue of their big populations being fertile breeding ground for all sorts of crimes. The narrative structure of a conventional gangster film is very straightforward. At the start of the film the audience will be presented with a young male character who is first becoming involved in 'low-level' crime – such as Henry Hill in *Goodfellas*, or Tom Powers in *The Public Enemy* (1931).*

As they become successful with low-level crime, these trainee gangsters rise through the hierarchy of the gang, becoming involved in bigger and more daring crimes. These young men rise to the point where they think they have it all. They meet their downfall

A youthful Henry Hill (left) being introduced to a life of crime by Jimmy Conway (Robert De Niro, centre) in Goodfellas

The Public Enemy – *scapegoats from other times*

usually by being killed or being sent to prison, but everything they have gained through criminal enterprise is taken away from them, providing a moral coda to these stories. When the conventions of the gangster film genre were being established with the early wave of gangster films in the 1920s and early 1930s, with films such as *The Musketeers of Pig Alley* (1912), *The Regeneration* (1915), *Little Caesar* (1931), *The Public Enemy* and the original *Scarface* (1932), these were times of economic hardship exacerbated by a wave of immigration into the US. The gangster film reflected these times and quickly built up some firm generic conventions – set in big cities, featuring young men who become enveloped in a life of crime, all seeking their own version of the American Dream of being able to make it 'big' on the basis of your own talent and hard work. These threads have been distinctly fused together again in the *GTA* series. All the games focus on men who are at the bottom of the social scale, who literally have nothing – no money, no possessions. In *GTA* games, you survive and thrive by using your own strength, intelligence, cunning and skill to escalate through the ranks of a criminal gang – exactly the same narrative process that is found in gangster films.

When you start to map the closeness in overall narrative structures between gangster films and the *GTA* game series, one reaction might be that this is shameless copying and displays a complete lack of inventiveness on the part of the game designers! However, it is not as simple or straightforward. Firstly, the essence of the gangster story can be found in any number of different places through history; stories of people who have too much and get too proud and conceited can be found in many different cultures, such as the Christian Bible – this story didn't suddenly emerge in the early decades of the twentieth century when gangster films started to become produced. Secondly, and more directly for us in a study of videogames, is the impact that this might have on the player. In some parts of the media, game players are inaccurately stereotyped as teenagers who have no knowledge or experience of life beyond what they experience through their games consoles. The reality is that game players come in all shapes and sizes – it is not uncommon to know adults in their 20s, 30s and 40s who own and play consoles and videogames. Also, whatever the age of the player, we all learn about the world from a wide variety of different sources. As we live in an age where the media are readily accessible to us – arguably a 'media saturated society' – there are many people who would play a *GTA* game and recognise that these staple conventions of the gangster genre are being employed. This gives the player a firm idea of how they are expected to play the game, setting aside their own moral stances about criminality. As players recognise the artificiality of the game text, then it becomes clearer to the player that the text is indeed a text – nothing more than an artificial construct and, as such, something to be played with. Therefore, players will recognise that a game is after all just a game. While the critics, who push the 'effects model' at media students and the public at large, attempt to scare us with the supposedly harmful effects of games, it is very obvious to those of us who actually play games that there is a big difference between game and reality – and game producers, by using intertextual devices which refer the text at hand to other media texts, are pointing this out and rewarding the cultural capital of sophisticated game players.

The second point to address in how it can be argued that the *GTA* games are sophisticated postmodern texts is derived from the cast of characters who inhabit these cities and the range of actors that have been employed (particularly since *Vice City* onwards). In the first *GTA* game, the player has a choice of four characters that can be played. It was earlier mentioned that one of those characters is called 'Travis', an intertextual reference to the central character in *Taxi Driver*, Martin Scorsese's exploration of the rotten underbelly of New York City.

Taxi Driver – A tour of the underbelly of Liberty City

The film deals with prostitution, pornography and alienation from mainstream society and there are distinct echoes, arguably conscious and therefore postmodern ones, in the *GTA* games of these themes. Again, this could be condemned as lazy copying, but also it can validly be interpreted as deliberate postmodernist referencing to allow the viewer to tune out of themselves and release their subjectivity and step into the shoes of the games' characters. Also, this process of taking on the role of a character allows the player a mental space in which to do things they would not do in the real world – again this is a deliberate tactic to clearly signal to the player that this is a game they are playing and not reality.

This process has only been embellished as the series has continued. The choice of a small range of characters with which to play has been abolished in favour of a character that you are presented with, such as *Vice City*'s Tommy Vercetti; and the calibre of the actors who have voiced parts of the games has increased significantly. Besides the increasing calibre of the actors what is most significant is their background. In Film Studies, we learn about how stars bring expectations to every role they play – with the level of sophistication that the *GTA* games are working at, this type of analysis of the role of 'stars' is now directly transferable to Game Studies.

Let's consider some of the established actors who have voiced roles in *Vice City*, such as Ray Liotta, Tom Sizemore, Dennis Hopper and Philip Michael Thomas. The character, or avatar, who the player inhabits in *Vice City*, Tommy Vercetti, is voiced by Ray Liotta. The significance of this lies in looking at Ray Liotta's film career. His breakthrough role came as playing Henry Hill in *Goodfellas* – a film in which, in conventional gangster movie style, a young boy goes from rags to riches, which is exactly the narrative arc of *Vice City*. Therefore, Liotta isn't just hired and then simply slotted into a role; he is cast, at least in part, for reasons of intertextual resonance. He is hired for the 'baggage' and expectations he brings to the role. Game players who know *Goodfellas* also know what Liotta brings with him from his iconic role as Henry Hill – the person of the hungry, young man on the make. With Liotta as Vercetti, this is another deliberate, conscious act of referring to another media text which again signals to the audience very clearly that this is a text, that this is a game. By doing so, Rockstar invite the game's players to set aside their own views of the various illegal and immoral actions required to succeed at the game and immerse oneself in this game world which the player is repeatedly reminded is not the real world. Also, the culturally sophisticated player is invited to feel pleased with their knowledge of these signs from different aspects of popular culture.

In addition to the 'kudos' that Liotta with his *Goodfellas* background brings to *Vice City*, the inclusion of actors such as Dennis Hopper – whose film star persona revolves around his irredeemable bad guy roles in such films as *Blue Velvet* (1986), *Speed* (1994) and *Waterworld* (1995) – rewards the cultural capital that pop-culture knowledgeable game players will bring to their experience in *Vice City*.

Given that *Vice City* is set in the 80s in Miami, this already tips a postmodern hat to the TV series *Miami Vice*, and this indebtedness to the influence of the show on the look and setting of *Vice City* is sealed with the involvement of Philip Michael Hall, who played Tubbs in the original television series, voicing the character of Lance Vance. Everywhere you turn with the characters you meet and interact with in *Vice City* you are engaging with some big names in the fields of popular culture – including porn actress Jenna Jameson playing Candy Suxx. For those *really* long in the tooth, Deborah Harry, of new wave group Blondie, one of whose biggest hits was 'Hanging on the Telephone', voices the role of the taxi controller – who obviously spends a lot of time on the telephone.

Miami Vice: *The epitome of 80's cool*

This process has only escalated in *San Andreas* – employing performers such as Ice-T, a rapper and actor, and part of the first wave of 'gangsta' rappers, who became a star in the early 90s alongside acts such as NWA and Public Enemy. He voices a character called Madd Dogg, a sly poke at Snoop Doggy Dogg, another gangsta rapper – the intertextual references keep coming thick and fast. Another role is voiced by Samuel L. Jackson, who played a minor role in *Goodfellas*, but is possibly most well-known for his role as Jules in *Pulp Fiction* (1994) – another media text which is completely full of postmodern intertextual references and inhabits a similar kind of criminal underworld as the *GTA* games. To be able to 'get' all these references you have to have a very wide and deep knowledge of popular culture – these most certainly aren't games for dummies.

Perhaps the hallmark of any good postmodern text is that if you don't 'get' any or few of the intertextual references, then this lack of knowledge, or cultural capital, is not held against you – regardless of your knowledge of popular culture anyone can learn to play the game. In the final analysis, your success at a game rests upon your skill of hand/eye co-ordination, your cognition speed, your knowledge of the game and its challenges, and usually a fair helping of luck (or a good set of cheat codes).

ACTIVITY 4.4

Task – Are videogame texts postmodern texts?

Objective – To develop and apply your knowledge of aspects of postmodernist theory.

What to do – Pick one game or game franchise that you know very well and work out whether it can be classified as a postmodern text or not. Things to consider – number and variety of genres that the game can be labelled as belonging to, number and type of intertextual references.

GTA IN THE DOCK

As befits a game series which focuses on criminal enterprise, and given the moral panic which surrounds the representation of violence in games such as the *GTA* series and others, it is perhaps fitting that *GTA* should be placed in the dock of a competent court to answer any charges brought against it. That competent court is the fictitious Court of Media Studies. In this section, to try and bring to life the criticism levelled at *GTA* games, we will do exactly that – press charges against *GTA* and cross-examine the game. The structure of the remainder of the chapter will be the cross-examination of an imaginary spokesperson for the *GTA* games (explicitly not an actual spokesperson for Rockstar Games) by a barrister prosecuting the case utilising the range of discourses that anti-videogame and / or pro-censorship groups in societies use against games, and drawing from the kinds of accusation that have been made of the *GTA* games in real-life controversies.

IN THE COURT OF MEDIA STUDIES

The metaphorical Court of Media Studies exists to interrogate media texts to discover what range of meanings it is possible to see in media texts.

Prosecutor: '*Grand Theft Auto*, you stand charged with being a gratuitously violent game, which corrupts the minds of the players of the *Grand Theft Auto* game series with the series' positive focus on criminal enterprise, and displaying blatant sexism and implicit racism. How do you plead?'

GTA: 'Not guilty!'

Prosecutor: 'Is it true that you promote violence in your games?'

GTA: 'No, I wouldn't agree that it is at all true to say that the game series promotes violence. To suggest that I promote violence is to say that I advocate violent behaviour being used against other people. I don't think there's any credible evidence that this is the case.'

Prosecutor: 'I find that a strange response. Allow me to introduce Exhibit A – the cover for *Grand Theft Auto 3*. The image on the front cover contains images of a number of very violent acts. Would you not consider that to be the promotion of violence?'

Exhibit A

GTA: 'No, I certainly wouldn't. It would be quite correct to state that a number of violent acts are being represented on the cover, but I would argue that this is purely a presentational device to enable potential customers to decide whether or not this game is for them. Furthermore, I would argue that the style of the artwork would preclude anyone from seeing this as an attempt of realism – the style is a clear signal to the audience that this is a *game*, that this is something to be enjoyed. It is most definitely not trying to present itself as factual documentary. What the style of the artwork says is that this is a larger-than-life game which takes its inspiration from real-world events, reminiscent of the style of the artwork to be found in X-Men, Spider-Man, Batman and Superman comics – all of which feature violent acts, yet no-one asks for *Spider-Man 3* (2007) to be censored. In fact, the reverse is more likely to be the case. Tim Burton's first *Batman* (1989) inaugurated the institution of the "12" certificate for films for cinema exhibition in the UK, as Warner Bros. lobbied the British Board of Film Classification not to brand it a "15". Some years later, the theatrical release of *Spider-Man* in 2002 paved the way for a further relaxation of cinema certificates with the introduction of the "12A", "A" for "advisory", thus allowing much younger children into the auditorium if accompanied by an adult.'

Prosecutor: 'My experience of playing *GTA* games is that it is impossible to do well and make progress within the game unless your avatar resorts to crime. For example, when playing *Vice City*, unless you commit crime – such as assaulting bystanders, carrying out carjacking – all that the avatar can do is run about the city without accomplishing anything. Surely the construction of the game design itself promotes violence as the most effective means of problem solution?'

GTA: 'Certainly within the game world, one of the most effective tools for problem resolution is committing violent acts. For example, it would be true to say that if you wanted to get some money, then one of the quickest ways of accomplishing that is to physically assault a bystander on the street. However, it can also be argued that we have in games such as this a classic "chicken or egg?"' situation – are these games causing a problem or simply a reflection of it? Is the world a more violent place, is our society a more intrinsically violent one precisely and only because of games such as this? I think that would be a very difficult case to prove. Arguably a close reading of the game could lead one towards the opposite point of view – that these games most definitely do not promote violence. Being violent only consistently brings rewards in *Vice City* the better you know the city and its environment – if a player takes the approach to the game to be as violent as possible to every other character they encounter, they will quickly end up 'busted' (using the parlance of the games) – therefore indiscriminant violence does not pay in this game and will quickly lead to the player's downfall.

The final point I would like to make regarding this issue of the promotion of violence is to state the point that this is a *game*. The style of marketing and the style of the game itself and the fact that this game, to be played, has to be accessed through a games console all point to the fact that playing any *GTA* game is not to experience the reality of a criminal lifestyle, and the players of these games are not "cultural dopes", as theorists such as Adorno and Horkheimer of the Frankfurt School would have us believe. They are not feeble minded morons, but people who enjoy playing games precisely because they provide a break, a diversion from reality. Also games such as the *GTA* series offer players a space to simply be someone else for a while. Because the games go to such great lengths to highlight that the player does not simply play the game as themselves, there can be no confusion as to the fact that these are games and they are not part of the real world. To suggest that players in general have problems differentiating between game world and real world is highly insulting to the players and over reliant on old, out-dated theory.'

Prosecutor: 'Do you think that the *GTA* games have had, or could have, a negative impact on people's fear of crime? In order to "win" or succeed at the game, the narrative structure in each of the *GTA* games requires the player to rise through the ranks of an organised crime syndicate and participate in many acts of violent crime. Given that many young people who play these games may not read about crime patterns from any other source, do you think it is possible that regular playing of *GTA* games could distort your understanding of levels of crime in society?'

GTA: 'Well, like any other media text, the *GTA* games reflect influences from what is going on in the real world. No text, no author is hermetically sealed from real-world events. There are violent crimes that happen every day in any society – and we reflect that reality in these games, but we do not construct that reality; people in the real world do. It is partly true to say that to succeed in the game the player needs to engage in a series of violent crimes. However, while many videogames have an over-determined narrative structure – whereby you cannot do anything or make any choices except for the ones the narrative structure and game design impinge upon you – one of the features which has always been lauded about *GTA* games is the relative lack of constraints of an over-determined, overbearing narrative structure. It is perfectly possible to play *GTA* games, and enjoy the experience of playing these games without working through all the missions you need to accomplish in order to rise to the top of the criminal underworld. For example, it is possible to enjoy the driving and music aspects of these games. You can almost create your own game-within-a-game by testing how many different types of car you can carjack and drive within a certain period of time. This is a point which is all too easily lost sight of with regard to how game players actually play games – too many people think you can simply read from the screen what the effects of that game are going to be on the people who play it.

It is my firm belief that the games are sufficiently well designed, and audiences are so sophisticated in dealing with media texts in this "media saturated society", that it is not likely that playing these games and engaging in the violent crime activities which are a part – but not the entirety – of the game will have a negative impact on players' fear of crime. I think we have to accord audiences and players more respect than what the question implies. I am convinced that players have a very clear sense of the difference between the game world and the real world, and the level and types of crime experienced in the game worlds of the *GTA* games bear no relation to the level and types of crime in your society.'

Prosecutor: 'Do you think it possible that playing *GTA* games could have a negative effect on players' longer-term attitudes towards violence? Do you think that *GTA* game players could be desensitised towards the effects of violence because of what they encounter in these games?'

GTA: 'Well, firstly allow me to say that I think there is considerable merit in the cultivation theory in the broader strand of media effects theory, which I think is implied in this question. This question assumes that players' attitudes and experiences of violence are solely derived from what they see and experience in these games – if only that were so. In my opinion, the world that we live in is an extraordinarily violent one. There are major conflicts occurring in all regions of the planet – nearly every day, you can watch the television news and see reports of bombings and shootings in Iraq, of armed conflict between Palestinian armed groups, of the state sanctioned execution of Saddam Hussein on YouTube at your leisure. By comparison to all of these events and the wired public's ready access to them, I think it is difficult to isolate games such as the *GTA* series and argue that these have some kind of unique ability to desensitise people to the effects of violence. Also to be borne in mind is the cartoon style of the art design in the *GTA* games. These games have not been designed for maximum photo-realism; rather they draw attention to their artificiality, not mask it. These are games and the violence experienced in them is so far removed from the nature of violence in the real world that I find it unlikely that anyone could feasibly argue that *GTA* games are corrupting people's sensibilities about violence.'

Prosecutor: 'The "heroes" or central characters of all the *GTA* games have been exclusively male. Would it be true to say that this is evidence that

the *GTA* games are sexist because of their exclusion of women from active roles within the games?'

GTA: 'There are two ways of approaching this question – firstly, to look at the output of other media and try to judge whether the *GTA* games are "better" or "worse" at the representation of women; secondly, to consider how much more or less sexist the *GTA* games can be said to be when compared to real-world social institutions.

In videogames such as the *GTA* series, what we essentially have are flamboyant, stylised stories which are meant to be enjoyed but not taken too seriously. Therefore our nearest media relation would probably be action / adventure films. In common with action / adventure films, the *GTA* series share a focus on male protagonists – as they also do with gangster films, Westerns, science fiction films and many other film genres. An evening spent channel surfing through music channels will reveal that many artists featured on these channels are male fronted bands and male dominated – female fronted bands and female solo artists are far less common. So, the record of the videogame industry and the *GTA* games in particular is arguably no worse than any other sphere of popular media culture. However, that is admittedly not exactly a glowing defence of our own position!

It is obviously undeniably true that the games are male-centred, but while I have stressed all along that these are games, that they are artificial constructs, we as producers need to perform a balancing act where we reflect enough sense of reality to attract the target audience demographics – this means having male characters as the avatars in which players inhabit. We operate in tough, competitive markets and have to produce products that will sell. Although I would concede that the critics such as Tuchmann who talk of the "symbolic annihilation" (Strinati, 1995: 180) of women in media texts can be reasonably applied to the *GTA* games.

Further, if you compare the representation of females in the *GTA* games we are arguably no worse than real-world social institutions – which have far more power and ability to shape people's lives than a humble videogame. The management of many schools and colleges, for instance, are dominated by men, as is the management of major media institutions – the BBC and Ofcom to name but two. So are the games more sexist than these groups? To reiterate the point made above, the power of social institutions in the real world to shape the destinies and lives of people is far greater than the power of a videogame played for a few hours at a time, to set aside.'

Prosecutor: 'Would you agree that the plentiful representation of women in games such as *Vice City* as "sex workers" is harmful both to the players of the game and to the standing of women in society?'

GTA: 'Again, this is a question about the context of the media and videogames within the wider processes of socialisation. To agree with this statement would be to imply that I think that the *GTA* games are one of the main agents of socialisation – that is to say that *GTA* games are one of the main ways in which its players learn about the world. When put this way, the argument begins to quickly crumble. In order to reach a thorough understanding of this issue, it would be best to put people's and game players' use of media in a wider context. It is highly unbelievable to think that one game is solely reliant for forming and shaping a person's ideas about gender roles, we have so many sources of "information" about gender roles thrown at us from age zero – from parents, grandparents, siblings, friends, toys, playgroups, school and, yes, the media in the form of television. Given that *GTA* games are age restricted titles – legally speaking, anyone who plays *GTA* games in the UK should be at least 18 years of age – I don't think the argument that *GTA* games are warping players' values about gender roles can be substantiated. It is reasonable to assume that anyone who is at least 18-years-old is already pretty far down the path in the formation of their beliefs and attitudes about gender roles. Accordingly, people may argue that there are many *GTA* players who are not 18 and playing the games whose attitudes and beliefs are capable of being formed and moulded are subject to manipulation by the games. However, it should be considered how these players get access to these games – retailers turning a "blind eye", permissive parents, parents who think it is fine for their child to play such games, illegal copying and trading of games. There are many links in the chain between game and player, enough for robust gate-keeping to be enforced, should people wish to prevent minors from playing the games. As Michael Corleone says to Senator Geary in *The Godfather Part II* (1974), "Senator, we're both part of the same hypocrisy." For every social problem, the so-called moral 'majority' wants a scapegoat – it would seem that *GTA* games and the wider videogame industry are to be this year's model.

The question seems to imply that the hypodermic needle model of media effects holds true, in that it implies that gamers can offer no input of their own and will simply take what they experience in game worlds and "copy and paste" it into the real world uncritically. In terms of a simple direct answer to the original question, no, I don't think the number of female sex workers in *Vice City* is ultimately harmful to the players and to the standing of women in society. To return to the point I have now made a few times previously, the games are precisely that – games, works of fiction, and I believe that the players of *GTA* games can differentiate between game world and real world.'

Prosecutor: 'Isn't the "Hot Coffee" incident – where it was found that some versions of *GTA: San Andreas* game for the PC and PS2 that you could control your male avatar so that you were invited by a female avatar "back for coffee" and subsequently, you could operate you avatar to have sex with the female character – one that completely undermines what you are saying? (http://www.cbsnews.com/stories/2003/06/07/national/main557477. shtm).'

GTA: 'Well, arguably, this makes the game part of the problem of sexism rather than part of the solution and this part of the game implies a sense of the male as sexual predator, which reflects and parrots the kinds of scenario which you would find in many different types of media text which pass the censorious lobby by without a word being said. Once again, this is another instance of different rules and standards being applied to videogames than other media, because videogames are the runt of the litter. Additionally, it also needs to be considered what the role of the media in society – as a harmful constructor of social reality or as a critically reflective tool for highlighting areas of sexism in western societies and an indictment of the players who choose to work through and enjoy the "Hot Coffee" scenario. What needs to be remembered is that in a game such as *San Andreas*, the player has a wide variety of choice in what to do in their playing of the game – this game does not work in a limited, linear fashion, the player is never forced to play through scenarios or mini-games within the overall game.'

Prosecutor: 'Would you agree that the representations of women may have negative repercussions on how male players will respond to females in real life?'

GTA: No, I wouldn't agree with that statement. To continue from where I left off with my answer to your previous question, I firmly believe that game players can differentiate easily and adequately between game world and real world and that the hypodermic needle theory is not likely to readily apply to how the target audience (over 18s) use media texts such as videogames. For instance, I would not expect that someone who is fresh from playing a *GTA* game and who then goes for a walk down the street would assume that all of the females he passes are sex workers – people's own everyday experiences of the real world would tell you that it isn't going to be so. Of course, I understand that embedded within this question is the notion that it is the game's lingering influences which may steer the player towards viewing women with contempt, touching upon the cultivation theory argument that the more often we are exposed to a set of messages and values the more likely it is that we are to take them on board and adopt them as our own positions. It would be foolish of me to say that this is categorically impossible – but there are many other cultural spheres where females are represented in a negative light. For example, the plays of William Shakespeare are embedded into the National Curriculum for English and Shakespeare is lauded as one of the leading lights of English literature. However, consider the representation of women in *Macbeth*, one of his most celebrated plays; Lady Macbeth emerges as a cynical manipulator who will do anything to achieve her goals – yet this play is studied by schoolchildren! No-one calls for the censorship of *Macbeth*; no court is convened to try the cultural worthiness of Shakespeare's plays.

Also, to state what is painfully obvious, the representations of characters in the *GTA* games are not really life-like. Yes, there have been huge leaps forward in the sophistication of the design of the games from to *GTA* to *GTA 3* to *Vice City* and on to *GTA 4*… but still, these characters aren't photo-realistic and look no more "real" than the characters in comic books (who also are not particularly progressive in their representation of gender roles).

As postmodernist theory has made inroads into academia, there has been a loss of a certain rational perspective. For all that it is far easier to access media texts in a range of sophisticated ways in a wide number of places in the twenty-first century, compared to the 1990s and compared to the 1980s, some things surely hold true – the gaps between game worlds and real world are still very sizeable, too sizeable to be ignored and for players to become so immersed in the game to "forget" themselves in the real world. The world of *eXistenZ* is not here yet!

eXistenZ – *'Play It. Live It. Kill for it.'*

Returning to the terms of the original question, do I worry that playing *GTA* may have some negative impact on how male players will interact with females in real life? No, I don't, because I don't believe that the media are a primary agent of socialisation. There are a vast number of other factors and events which have far greater impact on how we view males interacting with females than games such as the *GTA* series. When I consider how rape and sexual violence are used as part of the toolkit for fighting wars, this moral panic about videogames pales into insignificance. I think of how rape and sexual abuse were employed systematically in the wars of the former Yugoslavia – particularly in the conflict in Bosnia between Serbs and Bosnians. To implicate *GTA* within this wider spectrum of abuse of women is lazy, irresponsible and untrue. Harsh, degrading treatment of women by men certainly predates the launch of the *GTA* games, and the "hyper-real" representations of gender in the games pales into comparison to some of the horrific acts performed in the real world.'

Prosecutor: 'I'd like to examine another area of concern with regard to the range of representations in the *GTA* games – that of racial / ethnic stereotyping. If we begin by looking at the criminal gangs who feature in *GTA 3*, would you agree that the *GTA* games are promoting negative stereotypes of ethnic groups?'

GTA: 'Are the games racist because they represent ethnic minorities in criminal gangs? Or are the games simply reflecting the reality of organised crime? While 6 of the 7 criminal gangs that feature in *GTA 3* are made up from ethnic minorities, this doesn't make the game racist *per se*. This type of argument has been regularly used to beat gangster films with. Simply because certain ethnic groups feature in these roles does not neatly equate to a negative representation of those groups. *GTA* games are not documentaries of the real world; they are fictionalised, dramatised, heightened versions of it. There are undeniable influences from the gangster genre in film in the make-up of the ethnicity of the gangs of *GTA 3* – for example, the Leone family is a reference to the Corleone family of *The Godfather*. What should also be remembered is that each player comes to these games with their own value systems and codes, and this interacts with the open nature of the narrative of these games – you are not automatically forced into engaging in racist behaviour.'

Prosecutor: 'In *Vice City*, the lead character, or avatar the player inhabits, is called Tommy Vercetti and is voiced by Ray Liotta, an Italian-American actor, best known for his role in *Goodfellas*. Is this not a case of the game indulging in some easy ethnic stereotyping – that of the Italian-American as mafia "wiseguy"?'

Ray Liotta: Henry Hill / Tommy Vercetti

GTA: 'Arguably it is – but this needs to be seen in a wider context of the referencing systems that have already been acknowledged operate within the game. *Vice City* is consciously referring to other media texts – *Miami Vice* and *Scarface* most prominently – so it is within this grander meta-narrative that we should be exploring this question. In media texts generally, and specifically within gangster films and RPG games such as the *GTA* series, lead characters have been from ethnic minorities within America. In these narratives, the attainability of the "American Dream" – that through hard work it is possible to move from log cabin to White House – has been extensively explored and exposed as just that: a dream. Arguably, what is being done in the *GTA* games is a reinforcement of this message from gangster films that ethnic minorities and immigrants get a raw deal in comparison to the WASPs who dominate the upper echelons of American civic society. So, rather than condemning games such as these for promoting racist stereotypes, perhaps they should instead be applauded for passing on this critique of American society and culture to a new generation in a new context. Instead of lazily copying ethnic stereotypes from films, the *GTA* games are part of an attempt to expose the inequalities which are a feature of American society, and indeed a feature of all societies where it is small, disenfranchised groups who comprise the "underclass" in that society. This is not dumb games design but smart sociology lessons in action.

If you look at the biographies of characters you will surely agree that *GTA* does not promote or condone racism or negative stereotyping but attempts to undermine it. For example, the character profiles of Vic Vance and Marty Williams from *Vice City Stories* challenge the perception of the games you are drawing on. Vic Vance, an African-American character is a former soldier with an exemplary service record – he is one of life's good guys. He only becomes involved in crime as part of an attempt to support his family – arguably this is a critique of the whole mode of organising capitalist societies, not racist propoganda. Also, the implied whiff of "white supremacy" surrounding your line of argument is countered in the character profile of Marty Williams – this white American is one who regularly engages in domestic violence to sort out his problems on the home front. These are not the products of racist games designers but challenging, socially aware texts.'

Prosecutor: 'It is interesting that you refer to *Vice City Stories* to support your case, as the main characters of this game draw from a wide range of ethnicities to compose the game's vision of the criminal class of *Vice City*. Surely rather than these games being "smart sociology lessons" they are retrograde racist nonsense?'

GTA: 'With any media text, the way it is received is partly determined by the cultural status of its producer and the social perception of the industry from which it springs. I spoke earlier about how these games are being scapegoated – to borrow again from the lexicon of sociology, videogames are the new "folk devils" (Cohen, 1972) who are corrupting the minds of our children. Yes, the range of characters who comprise the criminal class who the player will engage with in playing *Vice City Stories* are made up from a range of ethnic minorities – but so are the range of characters that you encounter in the critically admired crime film *Heat* (1995).

With the case of *Heat*, you are talking about a medium which now has a certain critical ballast to support and champion the products of the medium. The film was directed and produced by Michael Mann, who has become one of Hollywood's most respected directors. There was no big outcry about ethnic stereotyping when that film was released – indeed it was near universally praised by the critics. Arguably, the difference between that film and *Vice City Stories* – which is influenced by the TV series *Miami Vice*, created by Michael Mann – is the status of the medium. Videogames are the runt of the media litter and are now being regularly scapegoated. Additionally, *Vice City Stories* is a *GTA* game from the Rockstar stable, who have also attracted criticism for games such as *Manhunt 2* and *State of Emergency*. The range of representations in *GTA* and *Heat* are not dissimilar – the one big difference is the status of the industry and the producers involved.'

Prosecutor: 'I would now like to focus attention on the power that videogames such as the *GTA* series have over their players. Would you agree that playing videogames can become addictive and harm a player's social skills through lack of interaction with real people in the real world instead of fictional avatars in game worlds?'

GTA: 'Running through the entire negative discourse about the effects that videogames have on players is this idea that playing videogames can become an "addiction" – and is likened to how people can become addicted to alcohol, nicotine and other drugs. Indeed, this strain of thought surfaces regularly in the mainstream media – it occurred in the "Virtually Addicted" episode of ITV1's current affairs programme *Tonight with Trevor McDonald* in 2006 and again in the "Is TV bad for my Kids?" edition of BBC1's *Panorama*, screened in June 2007. However, this assertion that playing videogames can become an addiction seems a bit excessive, to say the least. If we look at what the word "addiction" means, this should enable us to develop a better understanding of this area.

According to the Collins English Dictionary (3rd edition), "addiction" means "the condition of being abnormally dependent on some habit, especially compulsive dependency on narcotic drugs". Here lies the answer. Arguably it is lazy journalism to say that people become addicted to playing videogames as the definition of the word talks about *abnormal dependency* – in what way is it possible for people to become *abnormally dependent* on playing videogames? If you don't play *GTA 4* for a day what is going to happen to you? Are you likely to suffer physical withdrawal symptoms – shaking or vomiting, as is the case when someone abruptly stops taking some form of drug which their body and brain has become physically addicted to? The answer to that is, quite obviously, no. Players may feel a strong urge to play games, but their functioning as human beings does not depend on them having a daily "fix" of *GTA*, whereas if one becomes addicted to a narcotic drug such as heroin, your body may well start to rebel against you if you don't have your next fix. Drawing parallels between playing videogames and addiction to drugs is nonsense. Perhaps it is better to look at obsessive-compulsive behaviours and how people can fall into such behaviour patterns – as is the case with people who develop problems such as gambling or checking whether doors are locked or not. But then this pushes us into a different dimension of looking for the cause rather than trying to nurse the symptoms. Perhaps more time should be spent looking at why some gamers do spend a lot of time playing games rather than interacting with their family and friends – or perhaps this would open a can of worms about how our young people feel about the people in the world around them. It is far easier to unilaterally blame videogames such as *GTA* for society's ills.'

Prosecutor: 'A powerful point well made. However, surely you would acknowledge the merit of the "Killology" thesis as advanced by Lt. Col. Dave Grossman in such books as *On Killing* – the details of which can be found at www.killology.com, which is also reflected in the CBS news article, "Can a Video Game Lead to Murder?", published 6/3/05 which details the murders committed by Devin Moore in Fayette, Alabama USA, who killed three people, including two police officers on 7 June 2003. The CBS article argues that "*Grand Theft Auto* is a world governed by the laws of depravity". I'm much inclined to agree. Given happenings like this, surely the "Killology" thesis is unarguable and therefore we should ban games such as these?'

GTA: 'Perhaps we should be careful of laying the blame on videogames for this crime. The discourse of concern about copycat behaviour and particularly the concern about copycatting violent behaviour as experienced in media texts into the real world is long-standing and predates the era of videogames. With regard to this theory, the influence of behaviourism in social science is very sizeable. The influence of studies such as "Pavlov's dogs" (http://en.wikipedia.org/wiki/Ivan_Pavlov, accessed on 5/6/07) casts a long shadow over much theoretical thinking in this area. While there is much merit in this study and in some tenets of behavioural psychology especially concerning how all animals (including humans) can be conditioned into certain modes of behaviour, we need to be very careful of always relying upon this model for identifying cause for murders such as this. In previous answers, I have remarked about how we need to be more aware of the full role and potential impact that any media text can exert on an individual – are games such a rich a source of socialisation as to warrant being labelled the *sole* cause of such crimes?

Perhaps we should be looking at other areas too – at the other agents of socialisation which are *continually* at work, rather than those accessed by choice for an hour or two each day. We can't assume that videogames have led to horrific crimes such as this merely because the perpetrator may have played videogames that some elements of the more established media do not like. I would strongly suggest that what is really needed is much more focused research in this area before too many hard and fast judgements are made. It would seem to me that the implied theory which underpins Grossman's "Killology" thesis is behaviourist learning theory, of which the classic "Pavlov's dogs" study was a key influence. Whilst the Killology thesis seems to bring an "obvious" and "common sense" answer to the question posed by the CBS news article, I think what is actually needed is a great deal more thinking and detailed research about the range of media effects theories, perhaps through more longitudinal research which looks more at the possible long-term effects of exposure to ideological messages and values from a variety of different media forms and sources.

Furthermore, I would argue that this type of behaviourist theory underpins old media effects theory such as the notorious and all-too pervasive hypodermic needle theory.

This theory makes the assumption that the audience member is too weak and passive to resist the messages and values espoused by media texts, such as videogames, and all too readily assumes that the messages communicated by media sources are taken on board unquestioningly by those who receive these messages. This type of theorising also seems to inform the CBS article you cited – another reason why this source should be treated with a fair degree of caution. Therefore, I don't see this as evidence that this is case proven.

The same "blame game" that is now being played with games such as the *GTA* games and others is part of a much larger history of media texts being scapegoated and blamed for criminal acts. What is being lost sight of by blaming games is personal responsibility for your own actions – it is far too easy to say that games "make" people violent; ultimately, it is people who carry out violent acts in the real world, not videogames. If people think that there should be greater regulation on sales of games, then that's a whole different debate about classification, censorship, corporate responsibility and personal responsibility.

Besides the influence of behavioural psychology in this area, too much of this thinking relies on old ways of theorising about how the media affects the people who consume media texts. Embedded within this philosophy is the idea that gamers are somehow powerless to resist the messages and values that may be encoded within games – this type of theorising about the audience as passive and pliable, composed of "cultural dopes" is very old and arguably out of date even before the development of videogame culture. Rather than implying that gamers are "dopes" and "addicts" perhaps we should be looking more closely at how games interpret the game worlds they immerse themselves in and what sense they make of these game worlds, rather than it being continually assumed that games "do" things to people.

In *GTA*, you can steal cars, assault pedestrians, shoot at people and the worst that will happen to you is that you will get "busted" – that is, you will lose the money and weapons that you've accumulated and then you're back out on the streets again. In real life if you're arrested for those crimes, you are looking at a substantial spell in prison for your trouble, so the feedback mechanism in *GTA* is completely unrelated to what happens in real life. So for a variety of reasons I don't think the "Killology" thesis is the great answer that some commentators seem to think it is.

Furthermore, to answer the final part of your question on the case for censorship of games such as these, what needs to be considered is whether or not game producers and regulatory bodies such as the BBFC in the UK or ESRB in the USA should prevent millions of people around the world from enjoying playing *GTA* games because one clearly troubled young man makes reference to them? Surely one of the basic human rights is that of freedom of expression – are you suggesting rolling back civil liberties because one person who killed people made an allusion to life and videogames? This completely doesn't make sense.'

ACTIVITY 4.5

Task – Research into regulation and censorship across different media.

Objective – To learn about how different media forms have been blamed for social problems.

What to do – Working in small groups, work up a list of videogames, films and television programmes that have caused controversy upon release, or attempted release.

Next, run searches in www.google.com on these titles. Work through the search results to find out what kind of controversy these texts stirred up and what decisions regulatory bodies have taken about their supposed suitability for public consumption.

You could share findings with other members of your group and compile a list featuring media texts in different media industries that have experienced problems with their relevant regulatory body or with media and / or public opinion.

To take the work a step further, the results of the research work could be used as a platform for a group debate on the case for and case against censorship of the media.

Prosecutor: 'You've very consistently promoted the virtues of videogames in this cross examination. What good, then, do you think can be had from playing videogames beyond being able to enjoy the intertextual references and being able to show off your cultural capital?'

GTA: 'I referred earlier to the episode from the current affairs series *Tonight with Trevor McDonald* entitled "Virtually Addicted". This episode presented a "traditional" view of gamers as being essentially teenage boys who lack the social skills required to enable them to socialise with their peers and family adequately, and therefore take refuge in these other worlds. However, as I have stated before, we need to be taking a much closer and more detailed look at what level and quality of interactions are going on when gamer interacts with game. In all areas of life, in all stages of development, "play" is extremely important as an educational tool. Videogames are disparagingly seen as some kind of brain pollutant, when perhaps we should be looking at videogames from the reverse of this perspective. Videogames are not brain pollutants but brain *stimulants* and can promote learning in a variety of ways. Howard Gardner, a noted educational theorist, opined that there are eight different types of intelligence – logical, linguistic, spatial, musical, kinesthetic, naturalist, intrapersonal and interpersonal intelligences (www. thomasarmstrong.com/multiple_intelligences accessed on 12/1/08). I would argue that playing videogames such as the *GTA* games can promote learning to develop all of these different types of intelligence. For example, playing *GTA* stimulates logical thinking and helps to develop logical intelligence because of the puzzle solving element of navigating the game – the player has to apply real-world logic in terms of driving cars and learn what the effects of crashing cars are. This is arguably a good message to be communicating for many *GTA* players who may well be in the early stages of learning to drive or having recently passed driving proficiency tests. Whilst the games are pilloried for the representation of a variety of social groups, the games can help to develop intrapersonal and interpersonal intelligence by placing the player in a safe environment – out of the real world – where issues and problems can be worked through by how you choose to play the game. For example, if a player has a problem with anger management, arguably by playing games such as the *GTA* series they can learn that resorting to violent solutions to problems can only lead to greater problems and not solve the problem at hand. For example, I have learned through playing *GTA* games that if I assault a police officer, I can expect not to get out of the situation and can instead expect to find myself "busted", as the games say. A useful lesson for any game player to learn.

Also, playing any kind of videogame promotes kinesthetic learning. While you may be sat in your armchair playing the game, you do have to operate the game controller and your ability to progress in the game depends upon how well you can learn how to operate your avatar, which is learnt through routine practice and experimentation. In turn, this helps to develop fine motor control and hand-eye co-ordination. I would certainly say that playing videogames offers the player more opportunities to learn and develop in – crucially – different ways than sitting in an armchair and reading a book.'

Prosecutor: 'Are you really saying that videogames are a valid educational tool?'

GTA: 'Yes, I firmly believe that through playing videogames such as the *GTA* series one can develop different types of intelligence. I really don't accept the argument that videogames are played by "couch potatoes" not actively engaging their brains because they are playing videogames. For instance, if someone is reading a book there is little observable behaviour other than seeing their eyes move across the page and the turning of pages – yet no-one challenges the efficacy of reading as a learning tool. So we have to treat behaviourist- influence approaches to media effects with some fair degree of scepticism. Perhaps people need to take greater account about where learning takes place – we can learn from all sorts of situations in all sorts of times and places. We learn how to navigate shops and shopping centres by walking around them. Learning is a continual process and we can learn from anywhere, so there is no reason to think that videogames and the *GTA* game series are not tools which can be used for educational purposes. For example, the later games such as *GTA 3* and *Vice City* are arguably good basic driving simulators – you can learn some of the basics of how to drive and handle a car without putting you and others in a real world, and therefore dangerous, situation.

Besides the educational value of games, we should also bear in mind their cathartic use. Games such as the *GTA* games which feature acts of criminality and acts of violence are arguably offering a safe environment for blowing off steam. Playing videogames acts as a kind of safety valve where frustration is worked through and game players can emerge from a gaming session feeling better than what they went into in. This is surely the reason that many adult gamers come home from work and play videogames in the evenings – as a mechanism for unwinding from the stresses and pressures of working life. With reference to the *GTA* games, I would argue that these games offer a safe environment for the playing out of fantasies without having any of the nasty side effects of having these fantasies enacted in the real world. Videogames are not an agent of moral corruption anymore than any other play activity has been in the history of humanity. For as long as there have been human societies there have always been methods of entertainment and game playing. The only thing that is new and different about videogames is the mode of accessing the game.

Prosecutor: 'Final question – do you still deny the charges pressed against you?'

GTA: 'I absolutely do – for all of the reasons I have given above in my responses, but also one other dimension. No-one has to play these games; no-one is forced to buy them. *GTA* operates within a very competitive market. Yes, these games have good marketing campaigns which support their release, but no-one is frog marched into a shop and forced to buy a *GTA* game. You have raised many areas of concerns within the games but I don't believe that any of your assertions proves the case that these games are corrupting the minds of the players. If anyone buying these games for themselves or for someone else seriously believes that playing a *GTA* game is going to have a negative effect on you then, first of all, you need to stop and think about your own actions. But no-one is being forced to buy a *GTA* game; indeed the shelves in game shops are stocked with a vast array of titles of all types of genre – no-one is being forced against their will to play games like these which do feature violence and criminality. This is the operation of the free market mechanism in a capitalist society.

Consequently, it should be pointed out that if these games didn't sell then they would stop being made. Like any other aspect of the leisure services industry, the continued existence of the *GTA* series depends upon audiences buying these products. In a capitalist economy, it is an economic fact of life that it is survival of the fittest. *GTA* games will go on being produced while there is an audience for them. *GTA* games exist in the shape and form they do because they are very popular with their target audience – if the games started losing popularity and started selling less we would need to look at what could be done to improve the games. We are very sensitive to the requirements of our audience as without them we don't exist. Therefore, arguably, we are only selling people what they actually want to buy, so perhaps rather than blaming games for moral corruption there are other, more appropriate targets for this type of questioning. Similar to the film *The Public Enemy* and the rap group Public Enemy we are being scapegoated for far larger social problems. Unequivocally, *GTA* pleads not guilty to the charges presented.'

ACTIVITY 4.6

Task – What is your interpretation of this debate?

Objective – To consolidate your knowledge of videogames and how this media form interacts with aspects of media theory.

What to do – Having read through this section, work out whether you wholly agree with the GTA defence of the case, wholly disagree with it or you find that you agree with some parts and disagree with others. If you wholly agree, then you have made a preferred reading of this section. If you wholly disagree with it then you have made an oppositional reading. If you agree with parts and disagree with other parts, then you have made a negotiated reading.

Once you have decided what type of reading, or interpretation, you have made of this section, then, in conjunction with a group of students work out where your views on these issues coincide and where you disagree with each other. This should give you a first hand understanding of how different trains of thought interact and deconstruct texts.

Following this, you could write up a summary of the group's discussion for future reference about the discourses surrounding the interpretation of videogames.

CONCLUSION

Now that you've got to this part of the chapter you should have good idea about the GTA games and how you can bring an academic analysis to bear on the texts. This chapter has examined the following:

1. The features and developments of the GTA series. In the first part of the chapter the focus was on providing an overview of the entire GTA series, to construct a 'family tree' of the series to enable the reader to put the games into context and to understand the production contexts of the games. As a result, you should now know the sequence in which the games have been produced and released, and how different features have been added along the way. One of the most important milestones in the GTA series was the shift from 2-dimensional 'top-down' style games in GTA, GTA 2 and GTA: London, to the 3-dimensional, more 'immersive' experiences offered by GTA 3 and its spin-off and successor games. This change in style of game play, coming with the shift from PS1 to PS2 platforms, saw the popularity of the series soar.

2. The GTA games should no longer just be games to you, but you should now have a good idea of who the producers of the games are and what else they do and why they do it. This tracing of the ownership and control structures of the companies behind the games serves as a good short case study in the myriad

links between different media institutions in different media industries. As part of a process of synoptic learning about key concepts in Media Studies this should be a useful reference point when thinking and writing about media texts, media institutions and media audiences, and the ways in which these are all linked in the cycle of production and consumption.

3. The section on identifying genres and classifying texts should be of use to you in Game Studies specifically but also within your wider study of the media. The kinds of processes which academics (people) work through when classifying texts as belonging to one generic body or another are pretty much universal and common to different media forms. Additionally, the work of conceptualising the *GTA* games as belonging to a number of different genres should be of direct benefit to you in your wider studies – the nature of hybridisation is one that needs to be grappled with when studying television, magazines, film, internet, radio; in fact, all of the areas of the mass media!

4. The section focusing on how the *GTA* games can be considered to be postmodern texts should be of use to anyone wishing to find a navigable road into some fairly tough theoretical ground with postmodernism. There are many long and unusual words used when discussing postmodernism, but hopefully what this section shows is that labelling a text as 'postmodern' is not to say it is difficult to understand but that it is easy to understand precisely because we live in a society where access to media texts is very routine.

5. The long section of putting *GTA* in the dock will hopefully have illuminated many of the areas why games such as the *GTA* series come under attack from some groups in society and certain elements of the media. The first part of that section spent exploring approaches to the nature and range of the representations of gender, ethnicity and criminality will hopefully help you to be able to think about these issues when analysing other game texts and any other type of media text. The style of the construction of this section will also illuminate the various types of criticism which are thrown at videogames and ways in which these criticisms can be defended against and undermined – useful for analysing any area of Media Studies. The second part of the *GTA* in the dock section tries to bring to life the debate about whether videogames can actually be a force for good and a way of learning and developing intelligence and skills to try to counter the range of negative associations that exist with playing videogames. Also, this section should give you a ready made 'light touch' look at some of the media effects theories, and the strengths and weaknesses of these theories.

Altogether then, this chapter has covered a lot of ground which should be of direct benefit to you when going about an academic study of videogames and also help with your wider knowledge of Media Studies.

GLOSSARY – KEY TERMS

Academic

The development of new forms of knowledge, theoretical ideas of ways of thinking. An academic approach to videogames is one that attempts to develop a conceptual framework to describe the various ways that games are understood. Examples of academic approaches to games are narratology, flow and ludology.

Aesthetics

Emotional, sensory, subjective judgements made in response to cultural artefacts are aesthetic responses. These are matters of taste and style and are culturally conditioned rather than natural.

Avatar

The visual representation or embodiment of the game player on the screen.

Behavioural psychology

Perspective within the field of psychology, believes in analysing the human mind through observable behaviour. Leading proponent is B.F. Skinner.

Bricolage

A combination of different elements of different media texts brought together to make something new. For example, the programme *X-Factor* is an example of bricolage in action – part music programme, part game show, part cabaret.

Catharsis

To purify or cleanse yourself by releasing emotions or feelings. In relation to videogames the question is whether playing a violent game releases pent-up anger and frustration which in turn makes a person less likely to be violent or angry in the 'real world'.

Cognitive

Psychological information processing such as memory, attention, perception, action, problem solving and mental imagery.

Conditionality

The understanding of cause and effect: one thing is a condition of another. In a videogame this might be the knowledge that if a character stands on a key icon, a door will open. Conditionality is the essential premise of videogames, and this sets them apart from other media forms.

Cultivation theory

Media effects theory which argues that the longer and more often we are exposed to certain ideologies in texts the more likely it is we will come to take those values as our won values.

Cut scene

The parts of a videogame which require the player to be passive and over which one has no control (these are viewing / listening / reading experiences), and are usually skipped over after the first contact with them. Designers and players debate the merits of these parts of games – whether they help the player, understand the gameworld or act as a distraction and obstacle, breaking the flow.

Desensitise

The process where we become less affected the more often we experience phenomena – the more violence that we see on television, the less shocked we get.

Discourse

The ways in which we come to understand the world through ways of talking, thinking and writing that become dominant. Taking a step back to explore how we come to say what we do, believing it to be common sense, is called discourse analysis. There are usually competing discourses at work and in the case of videogames there are some popular discourses about the 'effects' of games that often circulate without any evidence. A key philosopher who wrote about discourse is Michel Foucault.

Edutainment

Videogames designed specifically for educational purposes, usually linked to particular elements of the curriculum.

Effects

The suggestion that people's behaviour is influenced or altered as a result, direct or indirect, significant on others or relatively unimportant, of exposure to media, is described in terms of 'media effects'. These can be highly specific – a person carrying out violent acts after playing a violent game, or broader cultural effects – the argument that young people are less healthy than previous generations and that playing videogames contributes to this.

Engagement

When we are engaged in playing a game, we are not just immersed in its world but also able to engage with its principles, rules, conditions and what is required strategically to succeed as a player. Engagement and immersion are mutually dependent to a large extent, but immersion involves a state of absorption whilst engagement involves awareness of the game context as well as the experience of being in the game's world.

Ergodic

An enhanced version of interactivity. An ergodic videogame requires the player to make the game happen – without the player, there is no text, so this is considered a higher level of interactivity than, say, voting for a *Big Brother* eviction.

Ethnographic

An approach to studying people by paying attention to the specific contexts that produce or influence their behaviour, values and responses to culture. To do this, ethnographic researchers tend to research from within social groups over a period of time.

Feminism

Political perspective which believes that power in societies is held by men and used to the detriment of women – the saying that 'it's a man's world' encapsulates feminist thought and the feminist analysis of what is wrong in society.

Flow

This is a state of mind which happens when we are involved in activity which is challenging but pleasurable and gradually harder over time, with incremental rewards and feedback. Like immersion and engagement, this is a concept which seems to distance videogames from other media forms.

Folk devil

See entry for 'moral panic' – the folk devil is the agent blamed for the phenomenon supposedly causing social dysfunction.

Game world

The fictional world and environment created by a videogame.

Genre

The classification of any media text into a category or type. Whether this is an industry practice, an audience expectation or a critical / academic labelling process – or all of these – is a matter of debate.

Hybrid

Two or more genres or forms combined.

Identity

Gauntlett's (2007) recent work on identity is the best source for a definition – 'we all have a complex matrix of ideas about ourselves who we are and what we want to be'.

Ideology

A set of ideas, values and beliefs. A dominant ideology is a set that becomes the norm and is thus seen as natural, neutral, common sense, the 'way things are' when in fact it is a set of ideas that might be challenged. Ideology is powerful when dominant in this way. Media texts can be seen to reinforce or challenge dominant ideologies, and audience responses to texts can be analysed in the same way.

Immersion

There are two forms of game immersion – perceptual (where the player's senses are dominated by the experience of being in the game) and psychological (where the player is drawn into the game world at the level of imagination). Immersion is, arguably, a slightly more critical state than engagement, but we wish here to resit the notion of passive immersion as immersion always requires an element of engagement.

Interactive

Where the player has control over what happens in the game. Unlike other forms of media, videogames (apart from cut scenes) are defined by interactivity, and this sets them apart. For this reason some academics believe Media Studies concepts that work for texts like films and newspapers do not work for videogames.

Intermedial

Videogames often refer to other forms of media text. When one text refers to another this is called intertextual, whereas intermedial describes a media form which relies on understanding of and experience of other media (for example, film and music) to make meaning.

Intertextuality

The process of consciously referencing other texts within a text.

Killology

A new (and contested) school of thought, which was invented by Lt. Col. Dave Grossman in relation to the psychological effects of military combat. Grossman argues that violent videogames act as training devices for potential murderers in our society.

Kinaesthetic

Active, physical, tactile, involving movement in space. Kineasthetic games are rapidly increasing, with the Eye Toy range and the Nintendo Wii.

Lifeworld

A term from phenomenology, this describes the parts of a person's experience which can be distinguished from the representation of it in the public sphere. It refers to our experience of living prior to reflective re-presentation or analysis, which is of course very difficult to describe.

Linguistic

The academic study of human language in its various forms. A linguistic approach can be applied to any social practice or range of social interactions.

Literacy

The ability to use and understand language. Traditionally associated with reading and writing text, but now extended to include media literacy and new literacies. With this extended definition, such forms of communication as videogaming, blogging, social networking, film-making and viewing, and a range of other newer media practices are included as forms of language to be learned and used. Being 'media literate' is now seen by the regulatory body Ofcom as a key aspect of citizenship.

Ludology

The study of play. Ludologists believe videogames are defined more by interactive play than they are by narrative and, for this reason, academic approaches to games should take play as the focus for study, and the structure and experience of play should over-ride the player's requirement to 'read' the story of a game.

Marxism

Political perspective which argues that power in society is located in the hands of a small minority (the bourgeoisie) and used at the expense of the majority (the proletariat).

Media Studies 2.0

Proposed by Gauntlett (2007) as a rethink of Media Studies in response to web 2.0, Media Studies 2.0 would, if accepted by Media Studies teachers, move away from a focus on elite producers and citizen audiences, and instead analyse ordinary people as creative producers of content, shared through the internet and in particular social networking.

Mise-en-scène

A French term – putting into the scene – which is used to describe the photographic nature of a frame – set, costume, lighting, make-up, gesture, props, colour. This makes up the visual atmosphere and creates a sense of authenticity as well as signifying mood and symbolic references.

MMORPG

Massively Multiplayer Online Role Playing Games, for example, Second Life or Club Penguin or Counterstrike.

Moral panic

A phrase coined by Stanley Cohen in 1972, this refers to overstated reactions to seemingly deviant aspects of popular culture, usually mobilised by the mass media. Clearly certain videogames have been the subject of widespread moral panics and they are often blamed for declining moral standards in general as well as specific cases of violent behaviour and tragedy.

Multimodal

A form of semiotics, multimodal theory attempts to understand the way that human communication mixes together a variety of forms and how it simultaneously represents, orientates by establishing relations between people and organises (to be clear). For a full account, see Burn and Parker (2003).

Narratology

The study of videogames as stories. This approach is derived from literary theory and from the study of older media such as films. Narratologists believe the traditional Media Studies concepts can be applied to videogames, especially theories of narrative.

Postmodern

Describes an approach to culture which sees all texts as being intertextual and meaning as mediated rather than representative of a state of original reality. Postmodernists believe that it is no longer sensible to describe media texts in terms of how they represent real life or events, but instead we should see reality as increasingly mediated, so the boundaries between reality and media-reality are blurred. The most famous postmodern philosophers are both French – Jean François Lyotard who described 'the postmodern condition' and Jean Baudrillard who said Disneyland was a good example of this blurring of reality and simulation, which he called 'hyper-reality'. Because of the way videogames immerse the player in a virtual reality this form of media is often described as postmodern.

Psychological

The academic / scientific study of the workings of the mind, including perception, emotion, behaviour, personality and interpersonal communication.

Remix culture

Describes how young people who are confident with new media technologies and social networking online are able to combine quickly and reformulate a range of information from different sources. In cultural terms, it is argued that this way of organising and reworking information changes the nature of literacy. If this is true, then those (older) people who accuse new technology of contributing to a decline in literacy standards are wrong and in fact, as Johnson (2005) argues, new media and culture are actually 'making us sharper'.

Representation

Students of media are taught that media texts do not present a neutral, transparent view of reality but offer instead a mediated re-presentation of it. The processes by which audience members come to understand media texts in terms of how they seem to relate to people, ideas, events, themes and places. This is a very complex idea as the reader of a media text will play an active role in constructing these meanings herself. At its most simple, it is how media texts are understandable. Videogames are more complicated as we play them and thus play a more physical role in the representations.

RPG

Role Playing Game is any game where you take on the role of a defined character.

Rule economy

Games are structured so that players need to learn how to operate within a set of boundaries with a range of rules and conditions – from picking up health as you move around a game world to remembering how to carry out certain moves at the correct times. This range of rules and criteria to remember are key features of a game's structure and they clearly distinguish videogames from other media forms.

Semiotic

Making meaning through signs and symbols, which are either iconic (they appear to be like what they represent), arbitrary (they are purely representational and do not look or sound like what they represent) or indexical (they suggest what they represent). Semiotics is usually associated with the work of de Saussure and Barthes, both French structuralist theorists concerned with how meaning is structured and how cultural myths develop.

Simulation

The deliberate artificial imitation of an experience, or a process, with the intention of making the imitation as close as possible to the 'real thing'. Often used for training purposes where it is not possible to access the real experience.

Sociological

The study of society and social interaction. It differs from pyschology which analyses the individual human mind. Sociology is concerned with studying what humans do together or between each other.

Transgressive

Pushing boundaries, forcing change, breaking rules, going against accepted practices or social norms, causing shock and outrage. Often threatening the established 'order of things'. A practice which transcends conventional approaches and either subverts these existing ways of working, or challenges their value.

Verisimilitude

The way that a text combines a range of elements so that the viewer or reader is able to believe in its reality. Even a text with no relationship to the real world will establish verisimilitude if it has logic, plausibility and makes sense on its own terms. For realist texts verisimilitude will rely heavily on authenticity. The logical, seemingly authentic world of a text. Not the same as 'realist', because every text has a logical, sensible world constructed through continuity, detail and recognition. So whilst we might not believe that aliens are ready to invade, *Independence Day* (1996) is believable because it constructs a coherent verisimilitude.

Virtual

Virtual reality describes a range of phenomena which can be defined as standing in for, representing, looking and feeling like, but not actually being real. Postmodernists argue that it is increasingly difficult to distinguish virtual reality from reality itself.

Web 2.0

The second generation of the internet, where, it is argued, the world wide web starts to take on the appearance of what Tim Berners-Lee originally envisaged. Defined by collaboration, social networking and the democratic development and distribution of content by ordinary people, for example, MySpace, YouTube and wikipedia. The term 'web 2.0' is accredited to Tim O'Reilly.

FURTHER READING

Here are the details of all the games, articles and books we have referred to in this book, so that you can follow these references up for your own needs.

GAMES

Ape Academy (PSP)

Beach Head (C64)

Charlotte's Web (Nintendo DS)

Club Penguin

Combat School (C64)

E.T. (Atari 2600)

Elite (C64)

Gauntlet (C64)

The Godfather (PSP)

Grand Theft Auto (PS1)

Grand Theft Auto 2 (PS1)

Grand Theft Auto London (PS1)

Grand Theft Auto III (PS2)

Grand Theft Auto Vice City (PS2)

Grand Theft Auto Vice City Stories (PS2)

Grand Theft Auto Liberty City Stories (PS2)

Grand Theft Auto San Andreas (PS2)

Grand Theft Auto IV

Grand Theft Auto: Vice City Stories (PSP)

Green Beret (C64)

Halo (XBox)

Manhunt 2 (PS2)

Medal of Honor: European Assault (PS2)

Nintendogs: Labrador and Friends (Nintendo DS)

Pac-Man (Atari 2600)

Paradroid (C64)

Pokemon

Pong

Second Life

Space Invaders (Arcade)

Spacewar!

Summer Games II (C64)

Super Mario Bros 4

Tennis for Two

Winter Games (C64)

BOOKS / ARTICLES

Adorno, T and Horkeimer, M, "The Culture Industry", in Curran, J, Gurevitch, M and Woollacott, J (eds.), 1977. *Mass Communication and Society*, London, Edward Arnold.

Anderson, C and Bushman, B, 2001. 'Effects of Violent Video Games on Aggressive Behavior, Aggressive Cognition, Aggressive Affect, Physiological Arousal, and Prosocial Behavior: A Meta-Analytic Review of the Scientific Literature' in *Psychological Science* 12 (5).

Barham, N, 2006. *Disconnected: why our kids are turning their backs on everything we thought we knew*. London: Ebury Press.

Benderoff, E, 2007. 'Cheating a real problem in Club Penguin's virtual world' in *Chicago Tribune*.

Bennett, J, 2007. '*Teaching and Learning in a MUVE. A social constructivist and game based model for learning in a 3D virtual learning environment*'. Paper presented to IMCL Conference.

Bernstein, B, 1996. *Pedagogy, Symbolic Control and Identity: Theory, Research, Critique*. London: Taylor and Francis.

Barker, M and Petley, J (eds), 2001. *Ill Effects: The Media / Violence Debate*. London: Routledge.

Bruce, C, 2002: *Analyse This!* In Media Magazine 2, London: English and Media Centre.

Buckingham, D, 2000 – *After the Death of Childhood: growing up in the age of electronic media*. London: Polity.

Buckingham, D, 2007. *Beyond Technology: children's learning in the age of digital culture*. London: Polity.

Burn, A, Carr, D, Oram, B, Horrell, K and Schott, G 2003: *Why Study Digital Games?* in Media Magazine 5 and 6. London: English and Media Centre.

Burn, A and Parker, D, 2003. *Analysing Media Texts*. London: Continuum.

Burn, A and Durran, J, 2007. *Media Literacy in Schools: practice, production and progression* London: Paul Chapman.

Burn, Carr and Schott, 2003. 'Why Should We Study Digital Games' in *Media Magazine* 5. London: English and Media Centre.

Carr, D, Buckingham, D, Burn, A and Schott, G, 2006. *Computer Games: text, narrative and play*. London: Polity.

Cohen, S, 1972. *Folk Devils and Moral Panics*. London: MacGibb and Kee.

Csikszentmihályi, M, 1996. *Creativity: Flow and the Psychology of Discovery and Intervention*. New York: Harper Perennial.

Dovey, J and Kennedy, H, 2006 – *Game Cultures: computer games as new media*. Maidenhead: Open University Press.

Egan, K, 2005. *An Imaginative Approach to Teaching*. San Francisco: Jossey-Bass.

Flatley, H and French, M, 2003. *Videogaming,* Harpenden: Pocket Essentials.

Feuer, J, 'Genre study and television' in Allen, R C, (ed), 1992: *Channels of Discourse, Reassembled*, London, Routledge.

Gauntlett, D, 2005. *Moving Experiences: media effects and beyond*. 2nd edn. Eastleigh: John Libbey.

Gauntlett, D, 2007. *Creative Explorations: new approaches to identities and audiences*. London: Routeldge.

Gee, J. 2003. *What Video Games Have to Teach Us about Learning and Literacy*. New York: Palgrave MacMillan.

Gentile, Douglas A, Lynch, Paul J, Linder, Jennifer R, Walsh, David A, 2004. 'The effects of violent video game habits on adolescent hostility, aggressive behaviors, and school performance' in *Journal of Adolescence*, 27.

Hoggart , R, 1961. *The Uses of Literacy: Changing Patterns in English Mass Culture*. London: Beacon Press.

Jensen, K, 2002. *A Handbook of Media and Communication Research: Qualitative and Quantitative Methodologies*. London: Routledge

Johnson, S, 2005. *Everything Bad is Good for You*. London: Penguin.

Kendall, A, 2008. 'Playing and Resisting: Re-thinking young people's cultures' in *Literacy*. In press.

Kermode, M, 2007. 'Wanna See Something Really Scary?' at http://www.channel4.com/film/reviews.

Kerr, A. 'Spilling Hot Coffee? *Grand Theft Auto* as Contested Cultural Product' in Garrelts, N, 2006. *The Meaning and Culture of* Grand Theft Auto. North Carolina: McFarland.

Kline, S, 2005. 'Countering Children's Sedentary Lifestyles: An evaluative study of a media-risk education approach' in *Childhood*, Vol. 12, No. 2.

Lacan, J, 1979. *The Four Fundamental Concepts of Psychoanalysis (Seminar 11)*. Harmondsworth: Penguin.

Lankshear, C and Knobel, M, 2006. *New Literacies; everyday practices and classroom learning*. Maidenhead: Open University Press.

Lister, S, 2006. 'Gory games that can warp your brain' in *Chicago Times*.

McDougall, J, 2006. *The Media Teacher's Book*. London; Hodder Arnold.

McDougall, J, 2007. 'What do We Learn in Smethwick Village' in *Learning, Media, Technology* vol 32 no 2.

McDougall, J and Duncan, M, 2008. 'Children, videogames and physical activity: An exploratory study' in *International Jnl of Disability and Human Development*, 7 (1). In press.

McDougall, J and Peim, N, 2007. 'A Lacanian Reading of the Study of *Big Brother* in the English Curriculum' in *Changing English*, vol 14 no3.

Marsh, J and Millard, E, 2000. *Literacy and Popular Culture: using children's culture in the classroom*. London: Paul Chapman.

Mitchell, A & Savill-Smith, C, 2004. *Computer Games and Education: A Review of the Literature*. London: LSDA.

Newman, J, 2004. *Videogames*. London: Routledge.

Newman, J and Oram, B, 2006. *Teaching Videogames*. London: BFI

Papert, S, 1994. *The Children's Machine: Rethinking School in the Age of the Computer*. New York: Basic Books.

Squire, K and Jenkins, H, 2003. 'Harnessing the Power of Games' in Education in *Insight* 3(1).

Strinati, D, 1995. *An Introduction to Theories of Popular Culture*. Routeledge: London.

Tapscott, D. 1998: *Growing Up Digital: The Rise of the Net Generation*. McGraw Hill: New York.

Toland, P 2004 'What are You Playing At? Representations of Gender, Race and Nationality in Videogames' in *Media Mag 7*. London: English and Media Centre.

Tyner, K, 1988. *Literacy in a Digital World*. New Jersey: Lawrence Erlbaum.

Wallace, W, 2006. 'More than a Game' in *Times Educational Supplement*: 6.1.06. London: Times Newspapers.

Wolf, J and Perron, B, 2003. *The Video Game Theory Reader*. London: Routledge.

Žižek, S, 2002. 'Welcome to the Desert of the Real' in Easthope, A and McGowan, K (eds) *A Critical and Cultural Theory Reader*. Maidenhead: Open University Press.

Collins English Dictionary (3rd edition), 1994, London, Harper Collins.

MAGAZINES

Retro Gamer Collection, Volume 1, 2007, Bournemouth, Imagine Publishing.

Edge Presents… 1, 2007, Bath, Future Publishing.

WEBSITES

www.wikipedia.org

www.amazon.co.uk

www.rockstargames.com

www.cbsnews.com

www.thocp.net/software/games/next_generation.htm

DOCUMENTARIES

'A Personal Journey With Martin Scorsese Through American Movies', BFI TV, 1995.

Virtually Addicted edition of 'Tonight with Trevor McDonald' originally transmitted September 2006 .

Is TV bad for my kids? edition of BBC1's Panorama originally transmitted June 2007.

INDEX

STILLS INFORMATION

The publisher believes the following copyright information to be correct at the time of publication, but will be delighted to correct any errors brought to our attention in future editions.